Surnames for Women

A Decision-Making Guide

by

Susan J. Kupper

McFarland & Company, Inc., Publishers
Jefferson, North Carolina, and London

929.4209
Rup

British Library Cataloguing-in-Publication data are available

Library of Congress Cataloguing-in-Publication Data

Kupper, Susan J., 1949–
    Surnames for women : a decision-making guide / by Susan J. Kupper.
        p.   cm.
    Includes bibliographical references (p. 141) and index.
    ISBN 0-89950-496-5 (sewn soft : 55# alkaline paper) ♾
    1. Names, Personal – United States.   2. Married women – United
States – Names.   I. Title.
CS2389.K87   1990
929.4'2'0973 – dc20   89-43654
                                                                        CIP

Manufactured in the United States of America

McFarland & Company, Inc., Publishers
  Box 611, Jefferson, North Carolina 28640

To Richard
my inspiration and support

Table of Contents

Acknowledgments

It is customary to end acknowledgments with gracious thanks to one's spouse. I will begin with thanks to mine. Without my husband, Richard Adams, I would have neither begun nor completed this book. He provided me with the original idea. Then, from the first draft of the questionnaires to the final draft of the manuscript, he provided me with emotional and financial support, love and encouragement, constructive criticism and positive reinforcement. However, in contrast with spouses cited in other acknowledgments, he neither made coffee nor typed the manuscript.

I would also like to thank several other people:

Helen Kupper, who read parts of the manuscript and gave me encouragement and useful comments.

Jay Smith, who gave me the benefit of his broad knowledge and his insights.

Joan DiLeonardi, Ph.D., who advised me in writing the questionnaires.

Members of the Triangle Writers' Group, who read most of the chapters and gave me invaluable comments and suggestions. Their support helped give me the impetus to complete the book.

All of the women who took the time to complete my questionnaires and made this study possible. I am grateful to them for sharing their experiences and feelings with me so openly and generously.

Introduction

"My name is so much a part of me that changing it would be akin to radical facial plastic surgery." So declared Neda Alper, a 42-year-old respondent to the survey about women's names upon which this book is based. This is a book about the choices and feelings expressed by Alper and more than 300 other respondents. It is a book about women and their names: why they chose them and how they feel about them.

Neda Alper perceives her name as an integral part of her inner self. Other women think of their names differently. Lania Groleau wrote:

> I really like my name a lot. The longer I use it, the more it becomes mine. My first name changed many times before I settled on its present spelling, and the name is still evolving.... I don't tell this to many people, but I have many different names. I use a different name according to how I feel, who I am at that moment. Certain names fit different moods or personalities better than other names. There are even one or two "secret" names—my very private ones that no one else knows about.

The core of one's identity, or a fluid and changing entity—what does a name represent? When the women in this book answered this question, their comments were diverse, interesting and sometimes provocative. They may be particularly interesting and useful to a woman who is considering either changing or retaining her name. She may be getting married or divorced, or perhaps she just doesn't like the name she has. Whether she keeps her birth surname, takes a husband's, hyphenates two names, or chooses an entirely new name is up to her, but the experiences and opinions of the women I studied may help her in making a decision.

I began this book as a study of women who had kept their birth names after marriage. Because I kept my name when I married, I became curious about other women's decisions to do so. My own reasons were simple: I just felt more comfortable retaining the name I'd had all my life and under which I'd earned my academic credentials. I found it interesting that this practice had become more common in the past 10 or 15 years. "Certainly it's tied to the growth of the women's movement," I thought. "Women will tell me that they're asserting themselves as people separate from their husbands." Other than that, I had no well-defined expectations of what I might find as I began mailing out questionnaires.

What I found was fascinating and wonderful. Almost every day I opened my mailbox to find women's stories, feelings, and experiences. Though I knew none of the women personally, they were willing to share a great deal with me. They were amusing, sad, opinionated, argumentative, articulate, and illogical — and I am grateful to them all.

In writing this book I have let the participants speak in their own words and tell their own stories as much as possible. At first I considered writing as an objective reporter and leaving myself out of it. But I decided that doing so wouldn't be quite honest. Both the survey itself and my organization and selection of the material from it necessarily bear the stamp of my biases. I have also added my own interpretations and comments when I thought they were appropriate.

Throughout this book I have used "birth name" or "woman's own name" to refer to the name that a woman received at birth. I have chosen these terms upon consideration of contemporary usage.

"Maiden name," the traditional term, is out of favor. It has quaint, Victorian connotations, and its meaning is archaic. As Mary Lassiter points out, the term "maiden name" assumes that a woman is a virgin when she marries. At this point, the assumption continues, she undergoes sexual initiation, which is symbolized by her change of name. "To a contemporary female ear," writes Lassiter, "[the term] has about as much relevance and application as terms like 'chastity belt' or *droit de seigneur.*'"[1]

Today there are two main views on what to call a woman's name. Some, like Susan Ross in *The Rights of Women*, refer to the "father's name," to emphasize that children are generally given their father's name at birth. Therefore, they say, a married woman who keeps her "birth name" is just retaining a male name.[2]

Others think that a woman's name *is* her own, no matter who else had it before she did. One good explanation of this point of view comes from Ruth Hale, founder of the Lucy Stone League. (Lucy Stone was

2

the first well-known American woman to keep her birth name. Since 1921, the group named for her has encouraged and supported women in keeping their own surnames after marriage.) In a pamphlet entitled *The First Five Years of the Lucy Stone League*, Hale wrote:

> We are repeatedly asked why we resent taking one man's name instead of another's — why, in other words, we object to taking a husband's name, when all we have anyhow is a father's name. Perhaps the shortest answer to that is that in the time since it was our father's name, it has become our own, that between birth and marriage a human being has grown up, with all the emotions, thoughts, activities, etc., of any new person.... It is true of both men and women that they create their own names, out of whatever they started life with, and that a compulsion to change them in adult life is as belittling to one as to the other.[3]

Other writers and scholars today share this interpretation. Priscilla Ruth MacDougall, an attorney who is an expert on women's names, carried it a bit further. She uses the term "own" name to refer to "the chosen name of the woman, regardless of the origin of the name." (It could be a name that she acquired at birth, at marriage, or from a previous marriage, or it could be a hyphenated or made-up name.)[4]

I agree with those who speak of a "birth name" or a "woman's own name." The fact is that everyone receives someone else's name at birth. Each person then has to make that name his or her own.

How the Study Was Conducted

I began the study by researching the history of women's surnames in America. I found, not surprisingly, that the issue of names has been an integral part of women's struggle for suffrage and other rights in the nineteenth and twentieth centuries. (I have included this historical background in Chapter 1.)

Next I wrote and distributed a questionnaire to determine the opinions and experiences of women today. Initially I recruited participants through small advertisements in the *Mensa Bulletin* and the Chicago newsletter of the National Organization for Women. I chose these publications because they gave me access to what I hoped would be well-educated but otherwise varied groups of women. I specifically addressed the ads to "Lucy Stoners" — women who had retained their birth names after marriage. Nevertheless, I received responses from women who had made a wide variety of naming choices.

My ad read: "Attention Lucy Stoners: Are you a married or formerly married woman who uses a surname other than her husband's? If so, would you complete a brief questionnaire for me? Please write to Susan Kupper, Ph.D. [My address followed.]" By asking each woman to refer me to others who might be interested in filling out a questionnaire, I expanded my participant pool through a "ripple effect." The combination of ads and referrals proved to be an effective approach, eventually resulting in 362 completed questionnaires.

I also distributed a brief separate questionnaire to the husbands of some of the surveyed women to determine their feelings about women keeping their own names. Seventy men completed questionnaires.

The response rate was gratifyingly high: 75 percent of the women and 59 percent of the men to whom I sent questionnaires returned them. Why did so many people respond? I speculate that when these women deliberately chose their names, they made a commitment to the subject, and therefore they probably have strong feelings about the survey topic. The husbands who answered evidently feel strongly as well. Quite a few women, and a few men, wrote that they enjoyed answering the questions or thought that the topic was important:

> Thanks! This has been an opportunity for me to sound off!

> I would like to see the results of the study. I know my own reasons but I have nothing to compare them with.

> I am anxious to receive the results of your study. I think this is important to both women and men, as sexual attitudes and biases often surface when the topic is discussed.

> I have been married six years, and for many years I haven't given much thought to my wife's decision to retain her real name. I was surprised how adamant I feel on this subject as I answered the questionnaire.

I also think that the response rate was so high, and the responses were so open, because I assured the participants that I would not use their names without their permission. Only about 20 of the names in the text are "real" — these are the unique or unusual ones that could not be changed without distorting their significance or meaning. I changed

4

the other names, but tried to retain the ethnic flavor or cadence of the originals. All other information about the participants — age, occupation, etc. — is reported factually.

When I began the study, I expected that many women who used their own names would identify themselves vigorously as feminists, even quite militant ones. I found that this was not the case. Only a quarter of the women I surveyed belong to feminist organizations — ranging from the National Organization for Women or National Abortion Rights Action League to local women's crisis centers — and most do not consider themselves active members.

However, their statements often indicated that they were strongly influenced by the women's movement of the past 20 years. Most frequently the movement helped these women to assert the right to their own names and to identities separate from their husbands, and to do so out of a sense of strength, independence, and pride in themselves. Two women, for example, wrote:

> I knew from the time I was 10 that I would never be anyone but Sally Horton. Despite family flak about following some traditions, I was encouraged to be independent.

> I go through spells where I think I'll get married, change my name, raise a family, and live the American Dream, and then questionnaires like this or plain old cold harsh reality wake me up and I remember how independent I really am!

A woman in her sixties declared:

> Being a staunch conservative means I am very pro-family in the traditional way. Being a conservative also means I'm a rugged individualist and don't feel bound by all traditional social usages if I think they are meaningless.

Probably the most striking discovery that I made from the study is the deep emotional attachment many women have to their names. I had expected that they would want to keep their own names for convenience, or to maintain a professional reputation, or for other rather straightforward reasons. But many women have a visceral need not to take "someone else's" name: They fear that if the label changes, the contents will change, too.

The Participants

The women who participated in this study are diverse. They live all over the United States, range in age from 22 to 67, have been married one to four times, have a wide variety of occupations including attorneys, social workers, homemakers, computer programmers, and secretaries, and have incomes that range from subsistence level to six figures. What unites them is their nontraditional use of surnames. About 75 percent of them, whether married or divorced, have kept their birth names; 10 percent have hyphenated their birth names and their husbands' surnames; and the remainder have used a former husband's surname or have created completely new names.

The age distribution of the women in the study is significant. Over two-thirds are between ages 26 and 35, and only a few are over age 50. It is my impression that more than 15 or 20 years ago it was unusual for a married woman to use a name other than her husband's. Women who married 20, 30, or more years ago would not generally have thought of keeping their names, or would have considered it socially unacceptable.

Those few women who did use their own names 30 or 40 years ago were mavericks. An attorney now in her sixties, who took back her birth name after being divorced, wrote, "Please remember that I started using my maiden name in the 1940s when few women mentioned equality or women's rights. At the time of my second marriage in 1948 I felt I was lucky to find a man who would share my feelings about identity and equal status."

During the 1970s, as part of a revived and vocal women's movement, more women began to examine their choices in a name. Hence, increasing numbers who have married since that time, who are now in their late twenties to mid-thirties, decided to use their birth names or to hyphenate their names. They constitute the bulk of the women in the study.

The women I surveyed are primarily urban or suburban. Though they span the United States, the states most heavily represented are Illinois, California, Massachusetts, and New York, plus the Washington, D.C., area. To some extent, this results from my methods of locating participants: I lived in Illinois while doing some of the research and drew upon some local sources. To a large degree, the distribution also reflects population densities in the United States — New York, Boston, and Washington on the East Coast, San Francisco and Los Angeles on the West Coast, and Chicago in the Upper Midwest. (The Sun Belt cities are less well represented.)

All of the women that I studied have been married, and 77 percent are married now. Most tended to marry first in their mid-twenties, a bit later than women in the general population. About a third have been divorced, and those who remarried did so most often in their early thirties, comparable to American women as a whole.

These women are not contributing in a big way to world population growth. Only about 47 percent of them have children, and of this group only 13 percent have more than two children. Though the proportion of women without children appears very large, some of the younger women in the group have recently married and may have children in the future.

Demographic studies indicate that it is becoming more common for well-educated and career-oriented women to wait until they are past 30 and established in their careers before they have children. In fact, if the group I studied is contributing to any population trend, it is to the much-publicized "baby boom" by women in their thirties. In a group with a median age of 32, over 15 percent have a child under age one. Several successful attorneys, for example, are now in their early to mid-thirties and have had their first child within the past year. A 34-year-old psychologist has two children under the age of three, and a school principal, 35, has what she calls "1¾ children," the older one two years old. A registered nurse who did not marry until she was 37 has a three-year-old and a four-year-old.

The women who took part in this study are well educated — nine out of ten have at least a college degree. Of these, 32 percent also have a master's degree, 11 percent a professional degree, and 11 percent a Ph.D.

Their occupations reflect this high educational level and probably are typical of any group of well-educated, fairly young women in the United States today. They reveal a wide diversity in careers, though the most popular fields are those that traditionally have attracted women: education, social service, and humanities-related areas such as art and writing. More women in the study work in education than in any other occupational area. Attorneys comprise nearly 8 percent of the total group. Perhaps this figure is only chance, or it may reflect the increasing numbers of women who have entered the legal profession in the past

10 years. Possibly because of the educational level of the participants, only a few are non-executive office workers, such as secretaries
or clerks, and none are "pink collar" service workers, such as wait-
resses.

Only 4 percent of the women indicated that they work at home as
housewives, homemakers, or mothers. This figure may seem low, considering the predominant age range of the group (26 to 35) and the fact
that 44 percent of those who have children have at least one child aged
five or younger. It is, however, consistent with the trend for women to
return to work while their children are still very young, because they
need the income, enjoy their jobs, or do not want to interrupt their
careers in midstream.

As a group, these women are not wealthy, but their incomes com-
pare favorably with all working American women. Over half earn at
least $20,000 a year. Very few (3.3 percent) earn over $50,000 annually;
these are mainly attorneys or high-ranking business executives. Their
husbands, too, have comfortable incomes. Almost 75 percent of the
men earn $30,000 or more per year, and 13 percent earn over $50,000.
Many of the husbands earn considerably more than their wives, as is
the pattern (like it or not) in the general United States population. But
a substantial number of women in the study (13 percent) have a higher
income than their husbands, perhaps because this group of women is
well-educated and career-oriented.

The 70 husbands who completed questionnaires have a profile
similar to their wives. Most are between the ages of 26 and 40, slightly
older than their wives. Judging from their occupations, they are highly
educated, for most are professionals (lawyers, college professors,
psychologists, engineers) or business executives. A warehouseman and
a treefeller are quite the exceptions.

This is not a book about all women. The people in the study speak
for no one but themselves. They are not a statistically valid sample, nor
can they be said to be "typical" of anything. I have sketched their collec-
tive portrait here just to give an idea of who they are. Whether this
book is read for information, for support, or just out of curiosity, it is
not the statistics of the participants that are important, but the choices
that they have made, the feelings that they express, and the stories that
they tell. Their voices form the heart of this book.

1. A Short History of Women's Names in America

In 1922 Emily Post's *Etiquette* stated, "A wife always bears the name of her husband."[1] The *New Bride's Book of Etiquette*, published in 1981, instructed a bride on how to change her name on bank accounts, Social Security records, etc., but added, "If you are keeping your own name, simply plan on continuing to use it."[2]

Over the past 100 years there has been significant change in society's attitudes toward a woman who keeps her own name. Even in etiquette — one area of our lives that is slow to acknowledge social evolution — this change is evident. The process has not been one of steady improvement, however. The movement to assert a woman's right to her own name has shared the fortunes of the American's women's movement as a whole. These fortunes have been uneven, sometimes taking a step forward, and at other times taking one or two steps back.

Nineteenth Century

Before the mid-nineteenth century, it was almost unheard of for a woman to use a surname other than her husband's when she married. Even actresses changed their names upon marriage. (Some did so several times, perhaps causing confusion among theatregoers of the day.) The well-known actress Ellen Tree, for example, began acting under the name Mrs. Charles Kean after her marriage in 1842.[3]

In the early 1800s, a married woman owned nothing herself. Even her clothes belonged to her husband, who could dispose of her property and earnings in any way he liked. Indeed, a woman literally belonged to her husband. In such a milieu, she would hardly have considered having a name other than his.

The decades that followed saw many improvements in the legal status of women in the United States. The Married Women's Property

Acts, for example, did much to alter women's position as their husbands' "property." First enacted in Mississippi in 1839, these acts soon spread to other states. They gave a woman the right to hold property that she had before her marriage, to enter into contracts and to sue and be sued on her own, to be gainfully employed without her husband's permission, and to keep the earnings from this employment. The acts were not panaceas, but they did help to redress some of the most flagrant legal injustices against married women.

At the same time that their legal position was improving, American women began to become more vocal on their own behalf. Some, such as Harriet Beecher Stowe and Lucy Stone, took an active part in both the abolitionist and women's rights movements. In July 1848, the participants in the first Women's Rights Convention, held in Seneca Falls, New York, adopted a Declaration of Sentiments that declared "all men and women are created equal." They also passed a series of resolutions calling for sweeping changes in the legal and social treatment of women.

The question of what name a married woman ought to use was not frequently discussed in the nineteenth century. There were far more pressing issues to confront, such as women's education, property rights, employment, and divorce rights. There were indications, however, that some women had thought about the subject. Those who signed the Declaration of Sentiments at Seneca Falls used their own first names, and without the title "Miss" or "Mrs." They probably did so in deference to Elizabeth Cady Stanton, the driving force behind the convention. She insisted upon being called by all of her three names, and did not like being referred to as Mrs. Henry Stanton:

> I have very serious objections . . . to being called Henry. Ask our colored brethren if there is nothing to a name. Why are the slaves nameless unless they take that of their master? Simply because they have no independent existence. They are mere chattels, with no civil or social rights. Even so with women. The custom of calling women Mrs. John This and Mrs. Tom That and colored men Sambo and Zip Coon is founded on the principle that white men are the lords of all. I cannot acknowledge this principle as just; therefore I cannot bear the name of another.[4]

The first American woman to assert publicly her right to use her own name, rather than her husband's, was Lucy Stone. When she married Henry B. Blackwell in 1855, she was 37 years old and a well-known lecturer against slavery and for women's rights. Her letters shortly before her marriage reveal apprehensions about losing her freedom and her own identity, but Blackwell, an extraordinary man for the day, assured her that their relationship would be an equal partnership. At their wedding they signed and read a protest against "such of the present laws of marriage, as refuse to recognize the wife as an independent, rational being, while they confer upon the husband an injurious and unnatural superiority, investing him with legal powers which no honorable man would exercise, and which no man should possess."[5]

When Lucy Stone married, she initially decided to call herself Lucy Stone Blackwell.[6] By July 1856, she began using only Lucy Stone, because it was the name that symbolized to her all that she had become through her own efforts: a college graduate, a lecturer, and a well-known spokeswoman for important social causes.

Her determination to remain Lucy Stone created some problems. She had to sign legal documents as "Lucy Stone, wife of Henry B. Blackwell," since judges and lawyers would not accept her birth name alone. She used the same approach when signing a hotel register while traveling with her husband. They thereby avoided the accusation of being "free lovers."

The thorniest problems occurred when Stone had to deal with government bureaucracies. In the spring of 1879 she tried to register to vote for a school committee in Massachusetts. (Women had been granted this right in April of that year.) When she was refused the right to vote as Lucy Stone, she replied: "My name is Lucy Stone, and nothing more. I have been called by it more than 60 years, and there is no doubt whatever about it. If the use of a foot- or cart-path 20 years gives the right of way, surely the use of a name three times 20 years should secure the right to its use. There is no law requiring a wife to take her husband's name."[7] Because of this case, the board of registrars made a general rule that "a married woman must vote bearing her husband's surname."

Throughout the remainder of her distinguished career, Lucy Stone continued to use her own name. It is for this decision that she is best known today.

By the 1870s and 1880s, increasing numbers of American women acquired an education, despite the prevailing notions that too much mental effort was harmful to a female's delicate system and limited brain. Some embarked upon careers, even in areas that had previously been exclusively male. For the first time, women were doctors, dentists, engineers, ministers, and lawyers. In many cases, however, recognition of their accomplishments was difficult because they had two or three or more names in the course of their careers. Antoinette Brown, for example, who was America's first woman minister, married and turned into Mrs. Blackwell. The first archaeologist to discover and excavate a Minoan town site did so under the name Harriet Boyd; following her marriage, her name became Hawes. The cumbersome results of name change are particularly well illustrated by Mary Morse Baker Glover Patterson Eddy. She wrote and taught about science and healing under several combinations of her own name and those of her husbands. It is under the name of Mary Baker Eddy, using the surname of her third husband, that she is known today as the founder of Christian Science.

Clearly the practice that the feminist writer Una Stannard calls "nominal polyandry" was confusing and awkward, especially for career women. Why, then, did they continue to change their names? First of all, society discouraged them from doing anything else. This phenomenon is now called "cultural lag." Although social conditions had changed to make possible increased equality for women, prevailing social attitudes still reflected the past.[8]

Many nineteenth century feminists were not interested in the issue of a woman keeping her own name, and at most suggested that she use her birth name as her middle name. Others insisted that feminists should concentrate upon the suffrage issue, and should not alienate potential supporters by emphasizing a woman's right to her own name. Even Lucy Stone did not appeal the Massachusetts Board of Registrars' decision in 1879. According to her daughter, Alice Stone Blackwell, Stone did not appeal because she thought her common law right to keep her name might not be upheld. She wrote very little about the name question, and kept her primary focus upon women's enfranchisement.

Many feminists also took their husbands' surnames because they as a group had been accused of wishing to destroy the family. They feared that a man and woman living together, married but using different surnames, would be accused of immorality, and of being members of the "free love" movement.

Despite some societal disapproval, a surprising number of women in the late nineteenth century adopted names that did not conform to the "Mrs. John Smith" pattern. The same options that are available to a woman today were available to a woman then: She could maintain her own surname as her middle name, use a hyphenated surname, use her own surname alone, or even invent a wholly new name for herself.

Some, like Elizabeth Cady Stanton, Carrie Lane Chapman, and Frances Hodgson Burnett, adopted the first alternative. Others used hyphenated surnames. Ida Wells, for example, a black journalist who wrote against lynching, married in 1895 and henceforth called herself Ida Wells-Barnett. Elizabeth Cady Stanton's daughter Harriot used the name Harriot Stanton-Blatch, and Virginia Clay-Clopton, an Alabama suffragist, combined the surnames of her first and second husbands.

A few of the most daring or independent women followed Lucy Stone's lead and kept their own names. Elisabet Ney, for example, was a well-known sculptor. She married Dr. Edmund Montgomery in 1863, but never changed her name. It was very important to her to maintain the name she had made famous. She and her husband never even publicly acknowledged that they were married, and when they lived in the small town of Hempstead, Texas, they were almost run out of town by members of the Ku Klux Klan, who thought they were "living in sin."

Women who did not have famous names at the time of their marriages also kept their own names. A Michigan woman, Martha Strickland, married Leo Miller in 1875, and remained Martha Strickland. She earned a law degree in 1883, and later became a prominent attorney in her home state.

A few women decided to use neither their husbands' nor their fathers' names, but to create entirely new ones. In 1875 Alice Chenoweth married Charles Selden Smart and became Mrs. Smart. Nine years later, however, she wrote *Men, Women, and Gods*, a book that attacked Biblical views of women, and published it under the name Helen Hamilton Gardener. She eventually took this as her legal name, and maintained it even after she married for a second time.

The only groups of women who fairly consistently kept their own names (at least professionally) in the late nineteenth century were actresses and authors. An actress generally kept a constant stage name,

13

though she might have had a succession of different names in private life. A similar nominal practice developed for a female author, although it was slower to come into widespread use than for an actress. By about 1880 an author usually continued to use the name under which she had originally published, despite subsequent marriages and divorces. E. Nesbit, for example, who wrote delightful children's books at the turn of the twentieth century, wrote under her birth name even after two marriages.

Certainly more women than one might have expected adopted unconventional names in the late nineteenth century. If one tends to think of the Victorian woman as quiet and submissive to her husband (except for a few strident suffragists), the women described above were the exceptions to this generalization. They were, however, unusual. The great majority of married women saw no reason for using names other than their husbands'.

Twentieth Century

American women's attitudes toward their names in the twentieth century have generally reflected the status and progress of the women's movement. At times when there were active feminist leaders and organizations, as in the pre-1914 period, some women kept their own names. In later decades — the 1920s through the early 1960s — the trend was reversed. Heightened social and legal pressures, combined with a less vigorous feminist presence, caused almost all women to become "Mrs. Husband" when they married.

Pre-1914. In the United States, the years before World War I were a hopeful period for women. More and more of them were high school and college graduates, worked outside the home, or entered the professions. (In 1910, a surprisingly large 8.6 percent of United States physicians were female.) Women became leaders in a variety of social and economic causes, from trade unions and immigrant assistance to socialism and anarchism. These women, whether they worked for specifically feminist causes or not, saw their efforts as a way to improve the status and welfare of American women.

In such an atmosphere, larger numbers of women who were involved in feminist activity or who were touched by it kept their own names. This was especially true in feminist centers like Greenwich Village in New York and the Hull House area in Chicago.

Henrietta Rodman, a New York feminist, teacher, and reformer, kept her own name throughout her career. She led or participated in a variety of causes to improve women's status, education, and employment opportunities. For example, Rodman was instrumental in getting the New York Board of Education to grant maternity leaves to married teachers. (Previously, the Board had not allowed married women to teach in the school system at all.) She also worked to lessen discrimination against women in university admissions, took part in Margaret Sanger's birth control efforts, and championed new methods of child raising and education.

Other feminists who kept their own names included Crystal Eastman, a writer, lawyer, and organizer who worked vigorously for causes including suffrage, socialism, and peace. She remained Crystal Eastman through two marriages. Neith Boyce, a Greenwich Village novelist whose work featured courageous and often unhappy heroines, maintained her name after her marriage to Hutchins Hapgood, and named her eldest son Boyce. Another Village novelist and playwright, Susan Glaspell, used her own name professionally after she married. Fola La Follette, daughter of Senator Robert La Follette and of Belle Case La Follette, a lawyer and suffragist, kept her own name following her marriage to George Middleton. They even listed both names on their mailbox.

These women, and others like them, were admirably successful and independent. Yet one must remember that they were exceptional; their attitudes and actions did not conform to those of society at large. Even highly educated career women were barred from professional organizations in the pre–World War I period. Most women who worked outside the home were in low-paying clerical or factory jobs. And not one American woman could vote.

After World War I, as historian June Sochen stated, feminists "remained a determined, although by 1920 a shaken minority. Their ranks were not enlarged; rather, the war depleted them. The staunch few continued to work for feminism during the flapper twenties but they remained few."[9]

It was still difficult for women to play any but the traditional, accepted roles. It was even more difficult for those who insisted on keeping their own names, which the established mores said they should relinquish gracefully upon marriage. It was for this reason that a group of women, led by New York journalist Ruth Hale, founded the Lucy Stone League in 1921. Its purposes were to inform the public that women could legally maintain their own names after marriage, and to establish this right with the governmental bodies and other institutions that had previously opposed it.

Initially, the League was quite successful, and within a few years established within New York State that a married woman could use her own name on a real estate deed, on an account with the phone company, on a joint bank account with her husband, and on her voter's registration. Publicity generated by the League's efforts encouraged women elsewhere in the United States to successfully assert this right, too. Prominent women in the 1920s who were "Lucy Stoners," such as Margaret Mead, Amelia Earhart, Fannie Hurst, and Edna St. Vincent Millay, also helped to make the cause better known.

The 1920s Through the Early 1960s. Many of these achievements were short-lived. Beginning in the mid- to late 1920s, and continuing as late as the 1960s, there was a legal and social reaction to the gains that had been made by the Lucy Stone League and others. The legal profession increasingly insisted that a married woman legally had to take her husband's name, and many states passed laws requiring her to do so.

An important case occurred in 1924. Dr. Marjorie Mason Jarvis, a physician who worked for the federal government, discovered after marrying that her name had been changed on her paycheck. When she complained, her complaint was referred to the United States Comptroller General, J.R. McCarl. He ruled that all married women who were federal employees had to use their husbands' names on the payroll, since these were their "legal names."

Through the efforts of the Lucy Stone League and the National Women's Party, McCarl's decision received a lot of negative publicity. Had Dr. Jarvis appealed, she very likely could have had it reversed. By this time, however, she was no longer a federal employee, so McCarl could not reconsider her case.[10]

A year later journalist Ruby A. Black brought up a similar issue when she applied for a passport in her own name. With the backing of the National Women's Party, she was grudgingly granted the passport, though it said, "Ruby A. Black, wife of Herbert Little." Responding to

16

cases like Jarvis and Black, and to the publicity that they generated, the federal government did allow married women employees to receive paychecks in their birth names after the mid-1920s.

By the 1930s and 1940s legal reactions were occurring in the area of voter registration. One case, *Rago v. Lipsky*,[11] involved Antonia Rago, an Illinois attorney. She practiced law under this name and continued to do so after her marriage. In 1945 she was told that she could not vote unless she re-registered under her husband's surname, because Illinois had a law that required a person to re-register when his or her name changed "by marriage or otherwise." (Illinois was not alone in having a law compelling a married woman to vote in her husband's name. Many other states had similar statutes, or subsequently adopted them.)

When Rago challenged Illinois' re-registration law, the court stated that according to common law, a woman's name changes to her husband's when she marries. In fact, this is not true, but the court based its statement upon misinterpretations of several cases. The main point in *Rago v. Lipsky* is that Antonia Rago was denied the right to vote in her own name.

A few cases provided more successful challenges to these re-registration laws. In 1941, Gertrude Bucher decided to run for office in Dayton, Ohio, using her own name. (Though married, she had never used her husband's surname.) Responding to a challenge from the local board of elections, she asserted her right to vote using her own name (*State ex. rel. Bucher v. Brower*).[12] Twenty years later, Blanche Krupansky made a similar argument—that she need not use her husband's name to run for public office and to vote (*Krupa v. Green*).[13] In both cases, the court agreed with the plaintiff, and stated that it is custom, not law, that a woman changes her name upon marriage.

Why didn't more women follow the lead of Bucher, and later Krupansky? First, most women at the time probably never heard of these cases, since neither was highly publicized. Second, even women who considered keeping their own names probably would not have been willing to fight for this right in court, especially when the risks of losing were great.

As recently as 1972, an Alabama woman, Wendy Forbush, was not allowed to obtain a driver's license in her own name, because a state regulation required her to use her husband's surname unless she got a court order to change her surname legally. She challenged the

17

constitutionality of this regulation, saying that it denied her the equal protection of the laws. (*Forbush v. Wallace*).[14]

A lower court ruled against Forbush, and stated that the law in question had been instituted for the state's administrative convenience and that it followed "a tradition extending back into the heritage of most western civilizations." The United States Supreme Court upheld this decision; the justices maintained that the Alabama law was constitutional, since there existed a simple and inexpensive method for a woman to change her name if she so wished. Neither court recognized the administrative inconvenience both to the state and to a woman if she had to register for a license in her husband's name and then re-register in her own name, after obtaining a legal name change. Nor did they acknowledge the inconvenience to a woman of having a driver's license in a name (her husband's) that she never otherwise used.

Social pressures, as well as legal ones, discouraged women who wished to keep their own names. In the 1920s the emancipation flaunted by the flappers was a superficial one. Though they appeared to rebel against the shackles of the past, they were not seriously concerned with improving their status as women. Most went on to marry and to lead lives much like their mothers'.

Women's rights groups became less militant during the 1920s. The League of Women Voters, which was formed from the old suffrage organizations after women obtained the vote in 1920, aimed to educate women to use their votes well, but no longer concentrated upon issues specifically affecting women. Women's groups also split over the question of an equal rights amendment, first introduced by the National Women's Party.

Some women who had originally been "Lucy Stoners" became discouraged by the obstacles that they encountered in voting, holding property, etc., or perhaps by the opposition of their husbands. By the mid-1930s, the Lucy Stone League was much less active than it had been ten years before. The next generation, the Lucy Stoners' daughters, did not emulate their mothers. In the '30s and '40s many women who had established careers in the professions or in public life using their birth names assumed their husbands' names after marriage. Clare Boothe Luce, for example, wrote plays and newspaper columns under the name of Clare Boothe, but when she ran for Congress in 1942 she did so as Clare Boothe Luce. She may have done this to make use of her husband's famous name as well as to prevent antagonizing voters. It is true that Frances Perkins, who became Secretary of Labor in 1933, used her own name, over the objections of at least one congressman. However, only her fame and status allowed her to do so; most federally employed women did not follow suit.

Economic and political conditions in the 1930s and 1940s were also not conducive to feminist activism. With the coming of the Depression, women were affected even more negatively than men. Not only did employed women work for wages that were considerably lower than men's, but they were the first to be fired. With a shortage of jobs, it was felt that there should be only one job per family. New Deal projects such as the WPA employed very few women at all.

During World War II American women experienced a temporary "liberation" as more of them entered the work force, often in previously male jobs. These changes in women's work patterns were part of the war effort and did not represent any basic improvements in women's status. The nation simply needed "Rosie the Riveters" to replace absent men or to staff expanding defense plants. When the men came home, many women were displaced from their jobs.

The end of the war had other effects upon women. People felt a great need to return to normal life again, and emphasized the traditional values of home and children. Many families flocked to new suburbs to pursue the American Dream: a single-family house in a clean, safe environment, where the mother stayed home and provided a "nest" for her husband and children. Despite the prevalence of these values, an increasing percentage of women worked outside the home: By 1950, the figure was 31 percent. However, they were employed primarily in positions traditionally filled by women, such as typists and secretaries, not in manufacturing or in the professions.

The postwar years, extending through the early '60s, are considered by many historians and writers to have been a rather grim period for feminism. Not all women were isolated in suburbia, trapped by the "feminine mystique," but it was not a time in which many women gave thought (at least not publicly) to improving their status. Even the Lucy Stone League shifted its focus from an organization encouraging women to keep their own names to one that opposed sex discrimination in general. Many League members who did maintain their own names did so only professionally, and used their husbands' names socially.

The late 1960s and early 1970s brought a new surge in activity for women's rights. In asserting their rights, American women became both more vocal and more organized than they had been since the campaign for female suffrage, perhaps more than they had ever been. The women's movement encompassed a wide range of ideologies and outlooks: radical fringe groups like Redstockings, more mainstream groups like the National Organization for Women, local women's health centers, informal consciousness-raising groups. As a result of their own participation in the movement, or through its coverage in the media, women became more aware that they could assert their own identities as separate from their husbands, lovers, or fathers. For some, maintaining or regaining a birth name was a way to symbolize individuality.

Mary Emily Stuart, for example, decided to keep her birth name after she married in 1971. After she met opposition in registering to vote and in obtaining a driver's license in her birth name, she took legal action. The eventual court decision was a landmark in American women's efforts to use their own names.

In 1972 Mary Stuart registered to vote in Howard County, Maryland, using her birth name. Soon after this, the board of supervisors told her that she would have to re-register in her husband's name (Austell) because the Maryland attorney general had stated the surname of the husband becomes a woman's legal surname upon marriage. Only if she obtained a legal name change, the board said, could she vote as Mary Stuart. She took the issue to court, but the Howard County circuit court ruled against her, asserting that by common law a woman's surname changes to her husband's upon marriage. Stuart's troubles increased when the Maryland motor vehicle administration heard about the case, and threatened to revoke her driver's license unless she used her husband's name on it.

But she didn't give up, and she appealed the ruling of the circuit court. In October 1972 the Maryland court of appeals reversed the circuit court's decision, and upheld Mary Stuart's right to vote in her birth name. The court stated:

> We have heretofore unequivocally recognized the common law right of any person, absent a statute to the contrary, to 'adopt any name by which he may become known, and by which he may transact business and execute contracts and sue or be sued. . . .' There is no statutory requirement in the Code that a married woman adopt her husband's surname. Consistent with the common law principle referred to in the Maryland cases, we hold a married woman's surname does not become

that of her husband where, as here, she evidences a clear intent to consistently and non-fraudulently use her birth given name subsequent to her marriage.[15]

Stuart v. Board of Supervisors of Elections of Howard County was an important case. In part because of its influence, since 1972 most states have confirmed a woman's common law right to use her birth name after marriage. This confirmation has come in the form of legislation, judicial rulings, or written opinions by state attorneys general.

Some people, such as the feminist writer Una Stannard, fear that these gains could be destroyed if "another cult of wife and motherhood" occurs in the United States. But she acknowledges there have been so many court rulings in favor of married women's rights to their birth names that states would actually have to pass laws requiring women to take their husbands' surnames at marriage. At present, at least, many American women are aware of their right to maintain or regain their birth names. As the practice becomes more widely known and better publicized, more women may begin to see it as a possibility and a choice.

2. Identity

A poster in my local post office asks in bold letters, "Changing Your Name?" The illustration shows the skin of an orange being peeled away to reveal an apple inside. Although the picture caught my eye, I found it strange, for it implies that changing one's name is like shedding a useless outer layer and emerging as a new entity. Actually, changing one's name, particularly at marriage, is more like donning an additional layer which covers up the person who was there before. Many women who participated in my study wondered how this change would affect them and were concerned that it might alter or obscure their own identities.

Most of us take our names for granted. Generally our parents choose first and middle names for us, add the family surname, and from then on, each of us is identified by that combination. Our names are not just convenient labels, though. In a deeper sense, they are part of who we are, important components of identity. They set us apart from others, and come to represent all that we have been and done. Juliet was right that a rose will smell as sweet if it's called by another name, but there is more to it than that. Just as the label "rose" has a set of particular associations for us, so does each person's name. For most of us, a name is a personal symbol, not to be relinquished lightly. Mary Lassiter has written in *Our Names, Our Selves*, "Our names are a part of ourselves, not superficial, like a hat or coat, but vital, like a limb or organ."[1]

Maintaining or Regaining Birth Names

Nevertheless, most women are asked to abandon their surnames at least once in their lives—to become Mrs. Husband. About three-quarters of the women I studied were hesitant to give up what they saw as a part of their personal identities, and so they decided to maintain or reestablish their own names:

When I married, I felt a sense of panic, of losing my identity. Retaining my maiden name was a way to assure that I did not just become "David's wife."

I am glad that I maintained my birth name — the idea of being married was threatening to me and using my husband's name would have made me feel as if I had lost my identity as an individual.

I feel "unmarried" (i.e., separate) when I use my maiden name; it contributes to that inner need to keep one aspect free and my own.

All of my life I had been "making" me. To change my name seemed to be starting on a whole new person as well as wiping out all traces of the "me" who had accomplished, made friends, existed.

Using my first husband's surname really made me feel like a piece of property and not a person. No one was more surprised at this feeling than I was, since all my life I had planned on being Mrs. Somebody eventually.

Variations on this last observation were common — 36 women stated that one of the reasons they maintained their own names was to avoid feeling like an appendage, like someone's property.

Several women mentioned that only after they married did they realize how much their names meant to them. A physician, who used her husband's surname for the first several years of their marriage, said: "I felt lost with someone else's name. When I first married I didn't think about it. Only later when I was uncomfortable, I changed back."

Marilyn Burke and Esther Steinberg explained how they felt:

When I married I did not know of any woman who used her own name after marriage. When I became aware that it was being done, I immediately wanted to regain my identity. I suppose it was also a case of not knowing what I had given up until I had already done it. I am not strongly vocal or combative so I also needed to know that it was possible for me to do it legally and without investing a lot of personal energy and resources to be one of the first to do so. I hope you understand what I mean. By the time I changed my name legally, it was easy even in provincial and traditional Nashville. In fact, since it is so easy, I am constantly amazed that more women don't do it.

When I was married the first time I used my husband's name and right after our wedding I wondered who I was. Changing your name is very traumatic. You're not you anymore, but a part of someone else.

Identity

As I read these comments in the questionnaires, I was struck by the fear, even disorientation, that some women felt when they considered giving up their birth names. They feared that if they relinquished their original names, they would "disappear," or would become different, lesser persons. For these women, their names are much more than symbols.

Divorce also made some women see the significance of their birth names. Elaine Grover-Martin, a Kansas City attorney, said:

> I retained my birth name as a middle name upon marriage and took my husband's surname as a show of solidarity. Upon divorce I hyphenated my birth name and my ex-husband's surname in an effort to put the emphasis upon my own identity/independence. I kept my ex-husband's surname solely because the children had it and I felt it would be comforting to them.

Other women wrote:

> After I separated and began divorce procedures, it was important to me to reestablish my identity. I chose to do this by I.D.s with my maiden name.

> After changing my name in my first marriage, divorcing and obtaining a decree two years later changing my surname to my maiden name, I decided I would not change my name again, even if I were to remarry. I appreciated the strong identity I had with my name; I was proud of my accomplishments and did not want to abandon my identity with the person who could claim such accomplishments.

jan gardner (sic), who was later divorced, wished to disassociate herself nominally from her husband, explaining that she didn't care to be tarnished by some of his actions:

> The subject of names became important to me as I began to realize how much your name affects the way others think of you. As long as I used his name, it was assumed that I agreed with him on everything — that I cooperated in and approved of his various asocial activities. Now, using my own name, I am judged only by my actions, my reputation. No one else can destroy my "good name." It helps me to feel like an adult, complete individual.

25

Creating New Names

Women who took wholly new names, or made significant modifications of their birth names that were not related to marriage, felt especially strong that their names provided an assertion of self, "a statement of who I am." Lania Groleau used her husband's surname and her birth-given first name when she got married. "Five years later," she wrote, "after my son was born, I decided that I wanted my own name — this came along with a deeper realization of who I was as a person and a greater feeling of personal strength. I wanted to choose a name for myself that said more of who I thought I was becoming."

Women who created all or part of their own names chose ones that had a personal meaning for them. Andrea Papilion said: "I chose the name Papilion (*papilio* — the Latin genus for butterfly) as a symbol of one seeking and spreading sunshine and beauty. The sunshine (warmth) is important to me as a humanist; the beauty to me as an artist."

Beverly Grace, who uses only her birth-given first and middle names, stated, "I was planning to marry, did not want to be Mrs. Anybody, did not want to use my first husband's name, or my father's. So I went to court and dropped all of them.... It is a way of saying I am my own person."

Mariel went one step further and uses only one name. She wrote that after her business failed, she had to start life over and reestablish herself. "I no longer wanted the association of my married name, which I had used for nine years after my divorce," she wrote. "I had the choice of two maiden names (my birth name and the name of my adoptive stepfather), neither of which I wanted to go back to. Inasmuch as my first name is rather unique, I decided to use only that."

Some women were never comfortable with their birth names, and so adopted names that they felt better expressed who they are. One declared that she "felt like a different person than those other names indicated," while another woman explained, "I have never liked my name — it was a name given to me by my adoptive father when I was two years old. It was an awkward, unusual name. In addition I did not feel accepted by my father's family and decided to choose a name with which I felt comfortable and connected — my maternal grandfather's name."

Melissa Cardozo plans to change her name soon to Robin Stephen. "I shall be very pleased to have a name of *my choice*," she said, "not one reminiscent of a bad marriage or unhappy childhood."

Identity Defined

The women who participated in the study have used the term "identity" in several different ways. At a time when most people use phrases from psychology rather loosely, it is not surprising that so many people referred to their identity or sense of self. By no means, however, does "identity" have the same meaning for all of them.

Some gave it the psychological definition used by Erik Erikson and others: an individual's identity is how she perceives herself in comparison to others within her society, combined with the way she perceives that those others view her.[2] One woman, for example, wrote:

> What was really important was that I worked so hard all through my twenties to know who I am/was, that I didn't want to be called by someone else's name. It was very important to finally feel (at 30) that I was glad to be me, and my name felt like it was connected to that precarious identity. I suppose if it weren't somewhat precarious, I might have been more willing to give it up.

When other women spoke of their identities, they meant a sense of self-worth — how they feel about themselves. A journalist who kept her birth name when she married said, "I think it grew out of my budding consciousness of myself as a woman deserving of respect as an individual." A young lawyer said, "I felt an extreme loss of personal worth, self esteem, and identity when I used my husband's surname for about one year after my marriage. I felt no reason not to change my behavior to make it consistent with my ideals and philosophies — so I took back my birth name and have always been glad for it."

On the other hand, some women defined their identities, expressed by their names, as the way other people see them:

> I come from a prominent, well-known family. Nobody knew who I was by my married name.

> My husband has a very strong personality. I felt to keep my "individuality" it would help to keep my maiden name. It was a statement to others.

Some perceived their identity as a sign or label for who they are: "After my second divorce," Gina Louterman wrote, "I decided that I did not wish to wear someone else's identity all my life."

Occasionally women used the word "identity" with more than one meaning. In the following passage, the writer first uses "identity" to refer to an individual's perception of herself within a relationship, and then uses it simply to indicate a means of identification:

> I feel strongly that women have enough problems not submerging their identities in relationships without stripping themselves of such a powerful component of identity and continuity with their past. What's more, my husband and I happen to have the same first name, which would have really compounded the identity issue!

However the respondents may have defined "identity," whether directly or by implication, it is an important concept for many of them. It is closely allied with the choice of names that they regard as "theirs," names that identify them to themselves and others.

Professional Identity

Physicians, attorneys, teachers, social workers, and others in the study mentioned another kind of identity — professional identity or reputation. About a quarter of those who answered the questionnaire stated that they had maintained their own names after marriage because they had established professional reputations under those names. Women in fields such as law and medicine almost all mentioned the importance of keeping a consistent professional identity for clients, patients, or colleagues. A lieutenant colonel in the Air Force Nurse Corps wrote: "I was older (37) when I married; I had established a career, records, licenses, credit, etc. all in my maiden name. I was 'known' by that name, which I felt would be good for my career."

Having the same name throughout their careers is also important for women whose professional accomplishments appear in print, e.g., writers, scientists, or historians. Leola Floren, a columnist for the *Detroit News*, continued to use her birth name professionally after she married. She wrote that she didn't want people to think that she'd "dropped right off the face of the earth (or perhaps into the sports section)."[3] A research scientist observed, "I had the example of several female colleagues who had switched names with each husband, leaving a very difficult-to-follow publication record. Having a clear record of publications is a must in my profession."

28

Identity

Sometimes when a woman and her husband work in the same field, the woman particularly wants to differentiate herself from her husband professionally by using a different name from his. Le Elen Miller, who took back her birth surname after 15 years of marriage, stated, "I did find it [the birth name] a decided advantage in business when my cinematographer/director spouse and I would be working on the same film for an industrial client (I'd do the script). In earlier years, we had found that clients seemed to regard one or the other of us as less professional, and sometimes felt that a husband-and-wife team should charge less."

Other women agreed:

> My husband and I are both economists. There is already enough potential for career competition between us. When I use my maiden name no one confuses our work and it may be slightly easier for us to both get jobs at the same institution.

> I am not my husband's possession, but his partner, and business partners have their own names.

Lee Krasner is a painter who was married to the abstract expressionist Jackson Pollock. She feels very strongly about having the name Pollock attached to her as an artist:

> I never used the name Pollock in connection with my work. I am Mrs. Pollock, but I've been Lee Krasner, I am Lee Krasner, and that name was used right through the marriage as well. The fact that people didn't know or didn't acknowledge it was their hang-up. Whenever people called me Lee Pollock concerning work, I had a fit. I don't want Lee Krasner Pollock; I don't want the name Pollock as an artist.[4]

One woman in my study had an unusual reason for wanting to have a name unrelated to her husband's. She wrote, "I decided to go to seminary to prepare for ordination in the Lutheran Church. It's hard enough for a woman to be a pastor; using my husband's Jewish name of Goldberg would have confused things hopelessly!"

3. Family Ties

Our families attract or repel us — but we need them. Some of us have a close bond with our birth families: We feel that family names identify where we came from and who our "people" were, and represent our kinship with those we love. Others dislike our birth families and try to break emotional and nominal ties with them — but soon we find ourselves forging new ties and creating new families of choice, rather than blood. As Jane Howard wrote in *Families*:

> Families as an institution, in one guise or another, will survive, because our need for them is so intense it approaches the genetic.... Our capacity and need to be part of one family or another — perhaps of several — is one of the thing that makes us human, like walking upright and killing for sport and bearing tools.[1]

The women in my study expressed this need for family identification repeatedly in their questionnaires. Many said that one of the most important reasons for using the names they did was to express ties with their families. This was often the rationale for retaining or regaining their birth surnames or for adopting other surnames that had family associations.

Women who feel close to their families stated that keeping their family names serves as an expression of these feelings. Geraldine Ferraro, the United States Democratic vice presidential candidate in 1984 (who was not in my study), is an example. She continued to use her birth name after she married, as a way of honoring her mother, who had raised the family by herself after her husband died.

Women in the survey stated:

> My parents (especially my mother) are proud of my career and my independence and I believe that the career and name somehow belong together. After all, my parents paid for all my years of education and I feel that they deserve some "recognition" which comes in part through my use of "their name."

31

The most important factor is that I come from a family of five daughters. We are very close-knit and we encourage each other to pursue all interests, no matter how far-fetched. Except for my husband, I do not feel at all close to my husband's family so I feel it makes more sense to keep my own name.

Though I've broken with tradition in one sense, I am preserving it — at least temporarily — in another. The world is amply stocked with Johnsons [her husband's surname]; Jarrels are an endangered species. Particularly since I am an only child, I'm glad to be able to keep a family name in existence for one more generation.

My family is Pennsylvania German, and from childhood I was patiently taught a number of "life skills" by various relatives — sewing, carpentry, gardening, reading, and cooking (well enough to now earn $14 per hour teaching cooking). My family heritage and family mean a lot to me and the name stands for something in my part of the country. Also, my father died when I was three, and I couldn't give my name up.

Several others also mentioned their father's death as an impetus to using their birth surname. Shirley Ables, for example, wrote, "Shortly before my marriage, my father died. I felt compelled to keep my name — that part of him that was still alive." Another woman, now in her fifties, who took back her birth name after she was divorced ten years ago, wrote: "I first took this step after my father died because this was something he had given me. Then I changed my name on everything because I wanted to be me."

In some cases, names have ethnic identifications that women want to retain. Laura Cheng of San Francisco wrote, "I decided to continue calling myself Cheng because that is who I am and who my people are. If I used only my husband's name (Ardmore), people who did not know me or meet me would not know I was Chinese, and I think that would be a loss."

A woman who lives in Chicago stated, "I feel very strongly about my ethnic background (Estonian) and my last name is Estonian. Taking my husband's name would have camouflaged my ethnic identity."

Davida Schlegman wrote that she wanted to keep her family name "because it means a lot to me emotionally, historically, and sociopolitically. My parents and all the surviving family members of their generation are Holocaust survivors, and I may be the only grandchild bearer."

Family Ties

Alice Jermyn made a different sort of choice to identify with her family. When she married for the first time she took her husband's surname, and kept it after she was divorced. When she remarried she decided not to take her new husband's surname, but her stepfather's. Alice wrote:

> My Pop has been a very special parent. He and my mother married when I was 18, and I felt an immediate bonding. He has been supportive of me without ever smothering me. He has demonstrated respect and belief in me, even when I felt none for myself. He has never tried to take my father's place. I chose my Pop's name because I strongly identify myself as his daughter, and receive a great deal of pleasure from this.

Some women continue to use their own names after marriage simply because they like their names, and see no good reason to change. Kit Carlson put it most forcefully: "I love my name (Kit Carlson, like Kit Carson, you know?). I didn't always feel so strongly, but when I started working for newspapers, I found it gave me a great identification level. Nobody forgets a name like that!" Michelle La Grande cited aesthetics as the reason for keeping her birth name: "My maiden name is lyrical: La Grande. My married name is a dud: Funk."

In some cases, women have uncommon names that they want to preserve. Sally Pailolo, whose surname is ethnically Hawaiian, wrote: "I liked my unusual name, and I wanted my name to continue through my children, since it is rare and my only sister may possibly change her name." Another woman stated, "I have an unusual family name that I spent a quarter of a century teaching people to spell and pronounce. I felt I had earned it."

Cathy Pekala found that there are advantages to having a distinctive name. She took her husband's surname (Brown) when they were married, but reverted to her birth name after a few years. She said, "I began to feel like a number. It's too common a name — my doctor had three Cathy Browns. Credit has been mixed up since my husband and I had such common first and last names."

On the other hand, some people prefer having an easily recognizable name. Janice Smith explained, "My maiden and current surname is Smith. When I married I used my husband's name because I thought I would enjoy a less common surname. This was a mistake. I disliked having to spell it for everyone. So when I divorced I resumed the use of my maiden name. I enjoy having a common name that I don't have to spell."

Martha Holmes Davis had a somewhat different reason for wanting to keep her family surname: she didn't want to lose her first name!

> I sat down and analyzed why I wanted to keep my own name before I got married, and I concluded that it wasn't so much the last name as the first. That probably sounds funny. Well, it's not that I like the name Davis so well. It's that I want to retain my own given names. If I agree to use Sims as my last name, then presto! I'm "Mrs. Christopher R. Sims"—an adjunct to my husband with no identity of my own. . . . If I retain my own last name, they can't take my first name away from me.

A few women created new names that related to positive feelings about their families. Kay Annchild, for example, chose her surname because she is close to her mother and wanted a name with a feminist tone. Karen Rose dropped her birth surname and just uses her first and middle names. She did this because "I wanted a woman's name, a name that had no male lineage. All names were changed upon immigration to this country, anyway, so they only went back one generation. Rose was my grandmother's name."

Some couples, such as Marni Politte Harmony and her husband, Peter, decided to adopt new surnames together to symbolize the unity of their marriage. Marni explained, "To our way of thinking, we were coming together as two individuals forming a new entity (there is a 'group soul' or group life we now create). In marrying, we acknowledged that. It seemed that choosing and taking a new name together — one that reflected the spirit and intention of our union — was a meaningful act."

Jan Gold and her husband felt much the same way: "We wanted something easy to pronounce, non-silly, and meaningful. 'Gold' is a good symbol for a marriage, and we like the name."

Both couples rejected the idea of a hyphenated surname and didn't want to use their original surnames because they were difficult to spell and pronounce. In adopting new names, it was not their intention to deny their families or their heritage; they wished merely to emphasize their own bond.

Elaine Korf and Howard Mann acquired their new surname in a different way: They combined their birth names. Before their marriage, he legally changed his surname to Korfmann; she then took "his" name when they married. They also gave their daughter this surname. This is an uncommon arrangement, and can work only if the surnames are appropriate. When two people named Kowalczewski and Schellenmeyer marry, a combined name is probably not an option!

When these couples adopted new shared surnames, they effectively identified themselves as nuclear families, but at the same time ended their nominal identification with the rest of their families. (Of course, women have done this for years when they took their husbands' surnames at marriage.) Because of this, some couples encountered opposition from their parents when they changed their last names. But the couples themselves were very pleased with their choices. Marni Politte Harmony wrote that the impact upon their marriage has been "only positive. We have loved having such a beautiful and meaningful name." Peter agreed: "As a creative act, it felt and feels wonderful."

Divorce

After some women got divorced, they felt a need to regain identification with their birth families. Forty-one women who completed questionnaires specifically mentioned that they changed their names to avoid keeping their former husbands' names, which often evoked painful memories. Many also felt that since the marriages were over, they no longer wanted the names that symbolized these relationships.

Most, like Angela Nicoll, took back their birth surnames. She said, "I wanted to use the name that was mine from birth and not one that was a by-product of a defunct relationship." Another woman stated, "Under my own name I earned a Phi Beta Kappa key, etc. etc. My husband put me down for eighteen years to make himself feel superior. I feel more competent and confident under my own name."

In some cases, women objected to "sharing" their last name with an ex-husband's wife. A television producer and host in the Northeast wrote, "When my ex-husband remarried—and there were two Mrs. Deutschmans floating around—I couldn't stand that. I had kept 'Mrs. Deutschman' even after my divorce only because it was convenient for my daughters to have a mommy whose name was the same. After that, I went back to my birth name."

A few women whom I surveyed chose to keep some family identification by taking the name of a female relative or ancestor. Abigail K. Alcott did this and injected a bit of humor into her name, too. She had been married three times and taken her husband's name each time. Finally, she said,

> I wanted a name that sounded attractive to me. I kept my own first name and retained my maiden name as a middle name. The surname I chose is my great-grandmother's (who also had the same first name as I). So I was able to honor myself, my father, and my mother's heritage, all at once. And I particularly like my new initials — AKA — not only for their symmetry, but because they refer to a police short-hand for "also known as." Given my three marriages and prior name changes, I thought a little light-hearted irony was nice. I really like my own name, for the first time in my life. I feel it suits me!

A young woman from Oregon, recently divorced, wrote:

> My ex-husband's name is very unusual, and excites much discussion and explanation. I didn't want to be explaining his name for the next 50 years. My birth name is patriarchal, a "_____son" name, and I had dropped it at marriage. So I have taken my middle name as a last name. It was my great-great-grandmother's birth name.

Similarly, Ann Mathes Patterson said:

> When I was divorced, I wanted to create my own name and still maintain my family identity. I decided to combine my maiden name with my maternal grandmother's maiden name. She encouraged my efforts to build a career and I felt that in this way, she could be a part of it.

Norma Goodwin Veridan and Katherine Lidtke-Scharf decided to adopt names that acknowledged the importance of both their fathers and mothers. Norma was divorced after 21 years of marriage, and didn't feel comfortable using her ex-husband's name. Since her birth name, Goodwin, recognized only her father's side of the family, she decided to pick a new name. She described the process:

> First I checked with my kids who were then twenty, eighteen, and six-teen. My son, the oldest, was at college so he was not closely involved. My daughters said, "Do your own thing, Ma, but we want veto power." I decided to put a list on the refrigerator and invite comments on my proposals. I remember thinking, "What do I do when there is a whole

world of possibilities to choose from?" I wanted a name that would show a relationship, but not just to the males on either side of my family. I had a mother, too, who was as strong, if not a stronger influence on my life as my father. So I chose their first names, Dana and Vera, and combined them. First trial, Danver, was shot down on the refrigerator: "Norma Danver, Student Nurse" or "Norma Danver, Her First Big Parade." Nope, won't do. The reversed and combined form Veridan passed the test with my daughters who were, and are, I believe, proud of me for doing something different and non-traditional that I believe in. My son also said it was fine with him.

Katherine Lidtke-Scharf wrote:

After I was divorced for the second time, I decided that name-changes in general, for whatever reasons, were a horrible hassle, so I chose to hyphenate my father's surname with my mother's surname (feeling that I am more like my mother than my father, feeling entitled to her name as a birthright, and feeling that she deserves some recognition for her contribution), and to never change my name again.

Negative Family Feelings

A few women in the study chose their names based on a need to disassociate themselves from their birth families. Marcia Dunn, Erica Rusterman, and Joanne Keats-Santucci, who kept their ex-husbands' names after they were divorced, all had reasons that related to negative feelings about their parents. Marcia wrote:

I still think I did the right thing at the time of my divorce. If I were not in a profession where my name is important for professional recognition, I think I would have changed it back to my maiden name. I have grown accustomed to my name by now and it has become a non-issue. Upon reflection, however, I realize that using this name is very significant as a step toward liberation from a domineering family and sometimes a sad reminder of the dissolved marriage and the alienation from my parents.

Erica said:

When I divorced, I remained in the same locale as my father and mother. I got the impression that they felt that I, as a divorcee, was a "fallen woman," and would soon start promiscuous behavior. Further, since they think they are a "well-known" family, everyone would know what "Jim's daughter" was up to. I put a stop to the whole thing by keeping my ex-husband's surname.

Joanne Keats-Santucci explained:

> I am getting a divorce and am changing my name again. The judges here in Texas won't let me go back to my original name so I'm taking the name of my daughter: Santucci. I am also at this time adding a name of my own choosing — one that means a lot to me — instead of my middle name. So my name will be Joanne Orion Santucci. I don't choose to keep the "Keats" because I've recently realized that all my father contributed to me was his seed.

Some women who use their husbands' names after they marry may also be motivated by the desire to make a visible break with their families. Michelle Farby commented, "Some of my friends who really had horrible relationships with their fathers seem to *need* to take on their husbands' names."

For many women, the most important factor in choosing a surname is family identification. For them, the question is not, "What name will reveal my identity as an individual?" but, "What name will show my family membership?" Laura Cheng and Sally Pailolo wanted to maintain the nominal ties with their birth families; Kay Annchild wanted to honor her mother; and Marni and Peter Harmony wanted to express the unity of their own new family relationship. They all wanted to show that they belonged somewhere.

4. Feminism and Politics

"After a decade of involvement in the feminist movement, I could not consider taking my husband's name, since that act originated as a statement of possession. In good conscience, I cannot support or reinforce by my actions that kind of statement." So wrote Marni Politte Harmony, who chose a new surname with her husband when they married. "For us," she added, "taking *his* name was not an option." Marni was one of many women in my study who mentioned the influence of feminism or the women's movement as a factor in keeping their names.

The principles of the women's movement today developed in the late 1960s and early 1970s, when the majority of the women in my study were nearing high school graduation, in college, or just beginning their careers. These ideas helped to mold them at a time when each was trying to decide, "Who am I?" and, "What kind of a person and a woman do I want to become?" Because these women were middle class, in college or college-educated, and oriented toward a career, they were the group to whom feminist ideas were most accessible at this time.

There have been two main directions in feminism since the mid-1960s, both of which were significant influences upon the women I studied. The first was the women's rights movement, which directed its efforts toward achieving equality for women in education, politics, and employment. The National Organization for Women (NOW), founded in 1966, stated as its purpose "taking action to bring women into full participation in the mainstream of American society *now*, exercising all the privileges and responsibilities thereof in truly equal partnership with men."[1] This statement is a good, brief summary of the women's rights movement of the past 20 years, which has used "mainstream" approaches such as lobbying and effective organization to achieve its goals.

The women's liberation movement was the other direction taken by feminism. Women's liberation leaders sought to go deeper than women's rights, to explore and explode society's views of women. They observed that both men and women saw women as inferior and as incapable of acquiring and wielding power. The first thing to do, they felt, was to change the way women felt about themselves. One medium for this was consciousness-raising groups, in which women explored their own experiences, to see how they had been affected by society's expectations and restrictions. These groups became very popular in the early 1970s. The ideas and issues that they raised spread outside the groups to other women who read or heard about them. The effects of these groups were often powerful, causing many women to feel a new kinship with other women and to feel anger against men.

Out of these consciousness-raising groups arose the insight that "the personal is political." Women found that the problems they had believed were simply their own personal problems were common to women in general. They began to realize that all women faced sexism in some form, from outright discrimination in education and employment to subtle but destructive "put-downs" by husbands, bosses, and society. As David Bouchier wrote in *The Feminist Challenge*, "'The personal is political' originated in a reaction against male definitions of politics as an abstract activity concerned only with institutional power, which effectively excluded from politics almost everything which concerned women."[2]

In the past 20 years the women's movement has concentrated upon fundamental issues aimed at improving women's lives and self-images. Whether a woman keeps her own name is clearly a secondary issue, one that many have seen primarily as an indication of other more important changes for women. Yet it is a topic that both women's rights and women's liberation leaders have mentioned, and they have recognized its symbolic importance.

The National Organization for Women helped to spread awareness of the subject as early as 1970. At NOW's national convention in March of that year, the members adopted a series of resolutions, one of which stated, "The wife should be able to keep her own name." In December 1973, *Ms.* magazine published three short articles about women maintaining their own names. (Shortly thereafter some traditional, mainstream publications recognized that people were interested in this topic. In May 1974, for example, *Time* had an article called "The Name

Game" and *McCall's* had one called "My Maiden Name ... Till Death Do Us Part.")

Two women in my study were directly affected by the information from NOW and *Ms.* Le Elen Miller said, "I did not know the possibility existed until I attended a NOW meeting in 1973 at which the program concerned use of birth names." And Susan Bateson wrote, "I read an article years ago titled 'Give Yourself Your Own Name for Christmas.' The gist of it was that historically women were men's property and therefore gave up their given names for this reason. This article first gave me the idea of keeping my name."

Feminist writers in the early 1970s also discussed women and their names, primarily to point out the inequities in traditional practices. In her book *Sexist Justice*, Karen DeCrow wrote:

> When I got divorced for the second time, I thought I should get back "my own name." What was that? My first husband's last name wasn't my name. My late father's last name wasn't my name. I thought of taking my mother's maiden name, but realized that wasn't her name, but her late father's. I came to the conclusion that a woman has no name.[3]

Gene Marine, who wrote *A Male Guide to Women's Liberation* in 1972, observed, "There is something almost magical about our names which is deeper than our own culture. Yet we insist that women surrender them, showing the extent to which they surrender themselves."[4]

Erica Jong, in an essay called "The Artist as Housewife," made a perceptive analysis of the reasons many women want to keep their own names:

> Naming is the crucial activity of the poet; and naming is a form of self-creation. In theory, there's nothing wrong with a woman's changing names for each new husband, except that often she will come to feel that she has no name at all. (All men are mirrors. Which one will she look into today?) So her first name, her little girl name, is the only one which winds up sounding real to her.... If women artists often elect to use their maiden (or even maternal) names, it's in a sort of last-ditch attempt to assert an unchanging identity in the face of the constant shifts of identity which are thought in our society to constitute femininity. Changing names all the time is only symbolic of this. It's only disturbing because it mirrors the inner uncertainty.[5]

41

Surnames for Women

In her recent book *Naming Ourselves, Naming Our Children*, Sharon Lebell emphasized the importance of women's names. This is not a secondary issue, she declared.

> The issue of what we call ourselves and our children needs to take its place alongside other fundamental feminist questions. You can't get more fundamental than names. As long as females' names represent us as being derivative of men, then the idea of women's identities being derivative of men's will be a functional part of society's collective psyche, and men will be perceived as being superior to women.[6]

When the women in my study discussed their reasons for maintaining their own names or creating new ones, many directly credited the ideas of the women's movement. Sometimes they had come in contact with these ideas through membership in large groups like NOW or in small consciousness-raising or discussion groups. Some also knew other women who had not automatically assumed their husbands' names. As Joan Kelly wrote: "Because I am a feminist, I disliked the social and legal connotations of using my husband's last name. If I had not had friends who had also kept their birth names, however, I doubt that I would have thought of maintaining my own name or would have had the courage to stick by my decision." Other women made similar statements:

> Some of my friends were marrying around the same time I did, and it had been a common topic of discussion for a while. Most of us had assumed that we would keep our own names on principle (i.e., it is unfair for the women to give up their names in favor of the men's).

> As a young person growing up, I decided that I would never marry and therefore always thought I'd have my maiden name. When I finally did marry at age 30 I had strong feelings about keeping my name that were strengthened by the women's movement and by people I respected.

> A strong influence in keeping my own name was the early divorce of my older, admired sister, who had to change back to her maiden name legally, though she had long been left by the man whose name she bore.

Some women saw their names as personal *and* political statements of their convictions about women's position in society and about marriage. Ann Martin, a pediatrician in her thirties, declared that she kept her name because she is "politically opposed to name changing as a form of subjugation."

Kay Annchild came to a realization about her name similar to Karen DeCrow's. She said, "When I took my birth name back after my legal separation, I realized that I was trading one man's name, my ex-husband's, for another man's name, my father's. I decided to use a feminist name by adding 'child' to my mother's first name."

Some women, in delineating their reasons for keeping their own names, expressed an ambivalence about marriage and how it might affect them. Their statements reflect the warnings expressed in the women's movement over the past 20 years: that women are dominated by men within marriage, and that women can best express themselves as individuals when they are autonomous from men. Adrienne Schellerman, for example, wrote:

> Keeping my own name is more in line with my view of marriage as (to quote Rilke) "two solitudes that protect, border and salute one another." I feel I am less tempted to want to "lose myself" in my husband, that it's a reminder that I'm ultimately responsible for my own existence.

Susan Magruder made a similar statement:

> My husband and I prefer to be as free as possible within marriage, and retain our individuality in every way possible, while sharing the joys of marriage and family. Different names heighten our sense of independence from one another.

Sara Kowalski, who is a college professor, married in 1972 after living with her husband since 1969. She explained her feelings about feminism and marriage at that time of her life:

> I'd like to emphasize how natural keeping my name was in the ferment of the 1960s, and how taking on another identity would have been the traumatic decision. The concerns of feminism and liberation seemed so easily congruent.... Women were raising name as an issue, and it seemed very natural. It fit into a general leftist orientation we had against the legal institution of marriage.

One younger woman used a similar rationale:

> A factor that influenced my decision was a basic dislike of the "marriage institution." I wanted to avoid as many stereotypes and outward

symbols as I could. I wasn't belonging to anyone.... The two of us planned to share, to maintain a sense of equal partnership and equal participation. Along with not changing my name, I decided not to wear a wedding band. It is a public statement which includes my right to divulge or not to divulge my marital status.

Two women stated that their decisions to keep their own names were not influenced by the ideas of the women's movement. But perhaps they were. Jean Sutter said, "I *did not* maintain my maiden name because of feminist, or 'cause'-related reasons." However, she did explain that one reason for keeping her name was "a growing belief that we *are* our names. I don't know if women should keep their names or be encouraged to change them. Maybe we should instead inquire whether people should *marry*. Our world is changing so rapidly." Louise Sara Connor wrote, "Even before registering any sort of feminist consciousness, I have always felt a combination of pity and contempt for women who call themselves 'Mrs.' followed by their husbands' names. I do *not* feel that I am a different person as a result of marrying."

Implications

Although the women I studied are addressing a specific issue — keeping or choosing their names — their comments about feminism have broader implications. As I read the comments, I was struck by many women's need to assert autonomy and independence, and by their uneasiness about "losing themselves" in their husbands.

Two factors seem to be involved here. First, women who grew up with the women's movement over the past 15 or 20 years often heard feminists describe relationships in terms of power: powerful men vs. powerless women. Some may even have experienced this kind of relationship themselves. Second, society told everyone — men and women alike — during this period that the individual, not the group, was the important entity. David Bouchier, in *The Feminist Challenge*, wrote, "The whole social atmosphere from which the women's movement emerged was one which exalted personal freedom and self-development, an atmosphere entirely alien to the restrictions and responsibilities of family."[7] The combination of these influences have made many women hesitant about commitment, especially marriage.

Additional perspective on this subject comes from Betty Friedan's *The Second Stage*. Friedan says that the first stage of the women's movement is over, having caused major changes in how society sees women and how women see themselves. It is time for a second stage, she urges, with men and women working together in a "new human politics." She worries that the accomplishments of the first stage have established a new mold for women, a *"feminist* mystique" to which women feel they must conform. There is an uneasiness among both older and younger women now, Friedan believes, because they are not always comfortable with the new images and expectations of women. "The new image which has come out of the women's movement cannot evade the continuing tests of real life," wrote Friedan. "That uneasiness I have been sensing these past few years comes from personal truth denied and questions unasked because they do not fit the new accepted image — the *feminist* mystique — as our daughters live what we fought for."[8]

I sense this uneasiness among some of the women in my study. Many are still caught up in the ideas and the imperatives of the first stage, in Friedan's terms. They are trying to be different from their mothers, fighting oppression, and asserting that they are appendages of no one. These ideas are not necessarily negative, but they can be limiting, if they cause women to fear commitment and vulnerability. As Friedan wrote, "Daughters moving ahead where mothers could not go may be, in fact, not so much in danger of being trapped as their mothers were as they are in danger of wasting, avoiding life in unnecessary fear."[9]

On the whole, though, the women's movement has been a strong and positive influence on the women whom I studied. Among other things, it helped them to gain a good sense of themselves as individuals, and gave them the idea of symbolizing this by keeping their own names.

Sometimes a woman's feminist decision to keep her own name can have a positive influence on others, too. A 29-year-old financial analyst who works for a very conservative firm remarked:

> I hate to admit it, but I get a kick out of the statement it makes to some of the older people I deal with. Of course, it does make a statement, but not the bra-burning feminist of the '60s one that they seem to expect. Finding a "normal" person like me who has done it may go a long way toward changing their ideas of what a feminist is.

5. Pragmatism

Most women who kept their own names explained this for reasons that involved their feelings: They wanted to maintain their identities or professional reputations, keep their family names, make feminist statements, and so on. Others, however, cited purely pragmatic reasons such as convenience, credit, simplicity, or even laziness. In some cases, they found it was just easier and more convenient for them to keep the names they were currently using than to make a change. Bridget Kranz, now in her second marriage, uses her first husband's surname. She said: "The non-traditional name just evolved. After the divorce (with a five-year separation), I discovered that everything, including my house, was in the surname of my ex-husband. It was easier not to make the changes — even after the second marriage."

Another woman who has been married and divorced three times simply stated, "I was sick of changing." Others who have had a rather tangled naming history agree. Maureen Allendorf, for example, used her birth name until she was 13, her stepfather's surname until she was 18, her birth name until she married at 22, her husband's name during her marriage, and her birth name after she was divorced at 26. When she remarried, she felt it was easier to continue to use her birth name. Lynda Marcus, who now uses her birth name after several name changes, wrote, "In four years my name has changed three times. My employer, who is very much a traditional person, made one small break in his traditionalism by requesting that when I marry again, I should retain my maiden name — he thought the situation was getting really silly."

Some women mentioned simple laziness, and said that it was too much trouble to go through all the paperwork of changing their names on records and identification.

> Frankly, there was a lot of laziness involved. It was much easier not to change my name upon marriage than to change it.

47

I had enough to do getting ready for the wedding without running around changing all of my credit cards, etc.

I ordered a couple thousand bank checks before I got married; I didn't feel like changing my credit cards, driver's license, etc.!

I kept my name because of inertia — I had been known by it for 30 years — and because I kind of liked it. It was unusual, compared to my husband's name of Davis.

For most of my adult life I've been known as Janis Johnson. In my business, my clients have always known me as such. I'm basically too lazy to go through all the hassle.

(These sorts of statements, however, were generally cited only as secondary factors in women's decisions. Usually, the primary factors involved more positive convictions.)

The desire to maintain separate credit was a factor for some women in keeping their own names; in fact, 14 specifically mentioned this. In a world of computerized data banks, charge cards, and electronic checking, having a good credit history is important. Before 1975 it was difficult for a married woman to establish her own credit history. Often only her husband's income was considered in decisions about loans, credit cards, and so on. An older woman in my study, who is a lawyer, wrote, "I found after my first divorce that Mrs. Him had credit, but I did not — I didn't want to go through that again." She now uses her second husband's surname even after being divorced from him and from a subsequent husband.

In 1975 the United States Congress passed the Equal Credit Opportunity Act, which prohibited discrimination in credit matters on the basis of marital status or gender. This law, along with some others, made it possible for a woman to have a credit record independent of her husband and to designate the name in which this record is maintained. (See Chapter 10 for more information on this subject.)

Some women in my study didn't seem to know about these laws, and worried about losing their credit histories. As a young businesswoman said:

To some extent, a woman loses rights when married. Financial information becomes "grouped." I am opposed to this. I kept my birth name for many reasons. One of them is that I want to maintain my own credit rating, which I had worked hard at keeping excellent. I want to be distinct from my husband, so that if I want a loan, I will be judged on my own. The "knee-jerk" requirement of a husband's signature on a loan application is not relevant to career women.

Another practical reason that women kept their birth names is the difficulty of tracing or contacting a woman who has married and changed her name. Though on one level this is simply a matter of convenience, on another level it is a more serious ideological issue. A journalist declared, "Imagine the fact that you can't even look up a married woman in the phone book unless you know her husband's first name! It is in these tiny details that the fabric of submission is maintained. Sounds strident — but it's true."

Other women observed:

> I started considering the need to keep my own name when working on a grammar school reunion committee; it was easy to trace the males but almost impossible to locate the married females (if no one kept in touch with them). When they changed to their husbands' names, it was as if they lost their former identity.

> I've lived in this town all my life. . . . When people who moved away "look me up," there I am. Had I changed my name, only people I am in contact with would know my new name.

> Since early childhood I remember regretting that I didn't know what my name would eventually be. It made no sense to me to change it. I like the fact that I can be found by friends from ten years ago by looking in the phone book — it seems strange that if I don't know a friend's "married" name, she's lost.

Several women chose their names for pragmatic reasons that were more unusual. Half in jest, perhaps, Terry Burger wrote, "My reasons were quite practical, actually. I am 5'1" and 92 pounds. My husband's surname is 'Small.' I work in a male dominated field and couldn't imagine attending conventions, seminars, etc. with my plastic name-badge reading 'Small, Terry!'"

The daily newspapers have occasionally offered stories of women who made decisions about their names based on practical considerations. Each of the women in the following two examples had a name that was well-known, though for different reasons.

In the first case, Bonnie Owens chose to keep a former husband's last name for more than one pragmatic reason. She is a singer-songwriter who has been married to and divorced from both Buck Owens and Merle Haggard. She kept the name Owens after she was divorced so that she would have the same last name as her two sons. After her divorce from Haggard, she thought about taking back her birth name, Bonnie Campbell. "I didn't want people to be always comin' up and talkin' to me just because I was married to Merle Haggard or Buck Owens," Bonnie said. "I wanted 'em to know *me*." But then she decided not to bother to make the change: "I thought, 'They'll just think I was married to Glen Campbell!'"[1]

The second example comes from Washington politics. In February of 1983 Anne M. Gorsuch, the head of the Environmental Protection Agency, was embroiled in a controversy over political favoritism and mismanagement in EPA's Superfund program. Then she got married. She dropped her first husband's name (Gorsuch), added her birth name (McGill), and took her new husband's name (Burford). Suddenly she was Anne McGill Burford, making her a less recognizable target. The *Washington Post* didn't care for this at all. In an editorial a few days after Burford's marriage, they complained, "In the midst of a grand Washington ruckus, with the cymbals crashing, the trumpets sounding and the hounds baying, the person at the center of it all has quietly gone and done a very unfair thing: she has changed her name. . . ." Furthermore, the *Post* huffed, "Mrs. Burford has availed herself of a refuge a male officeholder could never hope to use. But, of course men have no such respectable route as matrimony for escaping the notoriety their names have acquired."[2]

6. Feelings

Women who have chosen the names they use, rather than simply accepting traditional usages, have done so for a variety of reasons. They have explained the most important of these reasons in the preceding four chapters. Some provided philosophical or ideological explanations for their choices, while others gave more practical explanations. In most cases, their reasons were closely tied to feelings: Choosing their own names made them feel surer of their identities, closer to their birth families, freed from nominal identification with their former husbands, and so on.

Positive Feelings

One of the items that I asked on the survey questionnaire was "How do you feel about using your current surname?" About 80 percent of the women who answered this question stated that they had very positive feelings about their decision.

I love it. It's short, beautiful, distinguished, easy for people to remember. It's mine. I'm very proud of it.

I think it's a beautiful name — it is the name I was born to wear. It is the name that molded my life and since I am now who I was before I married, I see no reason to change what I am called.

Comfortable! Psychologically, it's mine. No one else's. If I marry again I won't change it. It expresses my relationship to my family — makes me feel much more a part of my heritage than another name would. It feels RIGHT. I love it.

Obviously I feel happy and comfortable doing what I am doing or else I would do something else. Perhaps because I made the decision so early (at about age 9) I have not intellectualized my decision or the ramifications of it; using my birth name seems so completely natural that I have never thought of advantages or disadvantages.

Most women considered that keeping their birth names or choosing their own names had a number of advantages, including a feeling of independence:

> I feel independent. I am not my husband's child or his responsibility and I will not adopt his name. His ex-wife is one of these financially dependent alimony-loving people — she can keep his name. That whole trip is crippling.

> I feel better (more independent) using my own name. I am unconvinced about the value of marriage as an institution — I feel a sense of freedom to have my own name. I think it also reflects an unwillingness to be subsumed by my in-laws.

> I feel I am an independent human being, not just a member of a marital pair. I feel it sets me apart from the typical suburban housewife (some solace during my full-time-at-home-mother period).

> I get a kick out of meeting people from the past and they say (to their spouse, for instance), "This is Ellen Edwards — or was." I say it still is and then explain. It makes me feel proud, independent, modern, like myself.

Many of the women whom I studied felt that when a woman's name is different from her husband's, she is perceived as separate from him. She is treated with more respect, both professionally and otherwise.

> My name has the advantage of identifying me as a distinct person and professional from my husband, who is also a lawyer. We are not first identified by colleagues as husband and wife and then as lawyers.

> It helps the world to see that my husband and I are partners and not in a superior/subordinate relationship.

> It gives me a definite advantage in business. I am treated seriously as an officer of the corporation by people I suspect would try to go over my head if they knew I was the boss' wife. My employees know we're married but most of my clients don't.

> Advantages are chiefly professional — I like working and publishing in my own name. I think it also fosters an image of independence and

ambition in the work place, which may be an advantage in the right circumstances.

People assume you *do* something if you have separate names, and there is less initial ignoring of wife. It gives people more information about me, and I feel a stronger social identity, more direct bonds to others.

I feel glad that I kept my maiden name. The fact that my husband and I have different surnames, I think, suggests to people that we have an egalitarian or "liberated" marriage. It's a suggestion we try to live up to.

Women who have regained their birth names or taken new names after being divorced appear to be particularly happy with their choice. They often feel that it symbolizes a break with their married life or helps to reestablish who they were before marriage.

I feel as though I belong to myself and have regained continuity with the past. The divorce was disruptive; getting my own name back was healing.

The advantage is really one of a psychological nature. I felt a certain loss of identity when I first married at 19 and lost my name. For 22 years I've wanted it back and now that I have it again, it feels like a struggle put to rest.

I am using MY OWN NAME. People tend to think I have never married (unless I specifically mention it). Then I can surprise them with the truth at my convenience. I do not feel I erased the mistake of marrying someone wrong for me, but I've corrected it, and I corrected the first name change.

I had a marriage that didn't make me feel good about myself (my ex was a very dominant person). When I began to realize what was wrong and try to work it out, I discovered that there wasn't much left to build a marriage on. In the process of discovering this, I began to develop self-confidence in myself as a person — a self-confidence that I had never had in my life. Because I initiated the divorce, I again had taken another step on my own. At that point taking back my maiden name was an obvious choice. My opinion on marriage is that a woman should keep her maiden name. I hadn't realized how much of your identity you lose by taking someone else's name — there are so many ways and means already set up in marriage to "put the woman in her place," without adding this to it.

53

Mixed Feelings

Some women who responded to the questionnaire had mixed feelings about the surnames they had chosen. The largest group among these were women who use hyphenated or double names. Most of them agree that their names are difficult to maintain intact because people tend to drop the first half. Gabrielle David-Barton, for example, wanted to keep her birth surname, but everyone in her small town assumed she'd take her husband's name. She compromised by using a hyphenated name professionally. "I've tried to use my double-barrel name socially," she said, "but in this small town my attempts are largely ignored and I turn up bearing only my first name and my husband's surname."

The very fact that a surname is two names strung together, women say, appears indecisive and implies that the name must have been a compromise. In many cases, it was. One woman confided, "I guess I'm still angry at myself for hyphenating at all — I really wanted to retain my own name, but decided to compromise to appease my husband and his family." Using a hyphenated name may be the only practical solution in such a situation. In only one instance in this survey did a husband adopt a hyphenated name along with his wife. As one participant remarked, "It irritates me that so few husbands of women with hyphenated names choose to hyphenate theirs — in such cases the situation remains unequal."

Women who hyphenated their names also found that other people considered their names to be confusing or cumbersome. Beth Kupper-Herr took her husband's name at marriage but switched to a hyphenated name several years later. "It's a bit long and awkward," she wrote. "A few people are puzzled by it. Since many people mispronounced my original name and my married name, they also mispronounce the combination. I prefer my current hyphenated name to just using my married name, but I'm still not completely satisfied with it."

Other women wrote:

> Although I feel proud of maintaining all of my family ties by using both names, it has been difficult — especially in filling out forms, receiving mail, or telling someone my name, particularly over the phone.

> It's much easier to keep a maiden surname or change to the husband's surname because no one wants to accept what they call "two last names."

It's a constant battle. Understandably, mine is a very difficult name to learn at once. I would not do it again—I would only use my maiden name. Hyphenated names are also clumsy and awkward unless they are very short or "WASPish" sounding.

Some women who participated in the survey disliked hyphenated names. Annette Ritter, who uses her birth name, had strong feelings:

I must speak out on hyphenated names! I abhor them! I think the only proper ones belong to old English families, e.g., Smythe-Jones. I can't tell which part is his, which hers, they won't fit on computer information forms, they're pretentious, and a poor solution to the problem of men's inflated egos.

But the consensus was not completely negative. Some women in the survey who use hyphenated or double last names felt they had made a good decision. Sandy Kramer-Lee said, "I don't really like husbands and wives with two completely different names. A company merger always includes some kind of agreement on a joint name. Why not a family?" Although Cathy Stone Wilson encountered some problems, especially when she first married and added her husband's surname to her own, she still believes that "the advantages are multifold. I love having a distinctive name. I think it is ever so much more dramatic than my old name or my married name would have been. It feels pretty and that was important to me." However, even these women agreed that hyphenated names involve extra explanation and confusion.

Some women, like Melissa Garvey and Elisabeth Kraft, have mixed feelings about having kept their birth names when they married:

I have given some thought during recent months to adding my husband's surname to my own name (that is, making my surname a middle name, and using his surname as the sole surname). As time goes on, and as we plan to have children, I feel less and less need to keep my birth name. I no longer feel (as I did seven years ago when I got married) that changing my name is a threat to my identity and an admission of inferiority. Now what concerns me is that using my birth name is inconvenient (just in doing everyday business with plumbers, etc.), and will be even more inconvenient when we have children who will use their father's surname. I feel no threat to my status, and if I hadn't established myself professionally using my birth name, I wouldn't hesitate now to change it. Right now I'm uncertain, because changing it would be a lot of trouble—but I think if I had it to do over again, I would have adopted my husband's surname when we married.

Until my daughter was born [wrote Elisabeth], I felt fine, even proud, to use my own surname. Occasionally around older people I felt uncomfortable about it, but mostly I felt that it makes a statement about my feminist beliefs that is readily understood by others. Since becoming a mother, however, I find I feel that a family should have one name for the sake of identity. The surname I have given my daughter (a hyphenated combination of my name and his) seems awkward, may be a burden to her, and consequently will probably not last through her lifetime. I wonder what name her children will have.

Sheila Rosen began using her husband's surname after initially retaining her birth name, but she, too, is ambivalent about this:

In the past three years, I have gradually adopted my husband's name for two reasons—one is that I have never liked or identified with my birth name and have thought of changing it to something else (grandmother's maiden name). The other reason, somewhat related, is that we named the children with my husband's name and, subsequently, I wanted to have the same name as they. In retrospect, if I had identified more with my birth name, I probably would have given the children a hyphenated last name and retained my own former name. You can tell from this brief description that this is a less than completely satisfactory solution for me.

Daphne Ellis took back her birth name after divorce. She is now living with a man and is pregnant. At this point she has many conflicting feelings about her name choice. Daphne wrote:

I'm a writer and editor, so I have a reputation (I hope) to maintain. Psychologically, although I love my former husband, I want no association with him in my name—only in friendship. As to my coming (?) marriage, I feel ambiguous because of my pregnancy. People will call me "Mrs." despite everything. But he has a wife (until his divorce is finalized) who hates me and it jars me to be called by a name I thought of as hers for years. I wonder how I'll feel to have a child with one name and me with another. I am the only one of my generation from either side of my family and have *that* tradition to carry on.

For some women, it was only when problems occurred with their own families that they had doubts about using their birth names:

Mostly I feel very good about it. I've always liked my name – unwieldy as it is! It gives me a sense of continuity with the past.... One thing that bothers me of late, however, is I've begun to wonder how much keeping my own name has to do with my attachment to my father with whom, until recently, I've always been extremely close. Since having a falling-out with him last year, it's crossed my mind several times to let go of his name and take my husband's just to make it clearer (to myself, mostly) that I've moved out of my childhood attachment to my father.... But every time this comes up, it's not as strong as the feeling that I want to keep the name I grew up with because it's my name....

Right now I have just returned from a fairly intense stay with my family. I'm wondering – why do I want to keep that name? It might be very liberating to separate from my family in this way! However, politically I believe in it and psychologically it's my name.

A few respondents did not feel strongly either way about their names:

It [her self-chosen name] does not seem like "a big deal" to me – I like it, I use it and so does everybody else. It was changed legally and is mine and that's that.

I would prefer never to have changed from my maiden name in the first place. (This is hindsight. I never thought of not changing it when I first married.) But having done that once, a name is just a name. I see no real advantages or disadvantages to it. [This woman continues to use her first husband's surname though she has now remarried.]

It [birth name] gives me my own identity. However, I do not feel so strongly that it is an issue with me. If my husband desired that I use his surname professionally as well as socially, I probably would.

Frankly, I'm not sure it's such an important issue. It seemed to be at the time I married. Now, though, I think independence or a healthy self-image is a function of self-confidence, competence, and a well-founded relationship. The name issue is incidental.

As I grow older, I care less what strangers, shopkeepers, my pediatrician's nurse, etc. call me. Many can't cope – they call me Mrs. Myname or Mrs. Hisname. I think, since I am certain about my own identity, that I am only sort of amused by what once might have seem a BIG ISSUE.

Should Women Be Encouraged to Keep Their Names?

Because most of the women who participated in this study are very pleased with the names they have chosen to use, many of them (45 percent) stated that other women should be encouraged to keep their own names or to choose another name. Another 50 percent said that they believed it was a matter of choice. (About 2 percent had no opinion on the matter; 1.5 percent did not answer; and 1.5 percent thought that women should not be encouraged to use their own names.)

"Yes! Women Should Keep Their Names!" Many of the women who took part in this study felt very strongly about keeping their own names, and did not hesitate to recommend it to others. One of the questions that I asked them was: "Do you think women ought to be encouraged to maintain their birth-given surnames after marriage or, alternatively, to take another name of their own choosing? Why or why not?" This question elicited some of the most forceful, even militant, responses in the study:

> I feel VERY strongly that all women should keep their own names upon marriage — or a name they choose. Personally I think husband and wife should both hyphenate their surnames or merge their names into a common surname (as a Klinebell and Bellman becoming Klinebellman).

> Women should absolutely retain their own names forever. Our own names are who we are, at a very deep psychological level. [In Alex Haley's *Roots*] the first act of Kunta Kinte's new owner was dubbing him "Toby" to establish him as property and to deny his previous self.

> Yes, to fight the idea of patriarchy. To make a public statement for equality. To discourage men from all thoughts, however slight, of dominance. And perhaps most important — to allow women an independent identity.

> I think anybody who undergoes a name-change without overwhelming reason is ignorant of the difficulties involved with changing identities, or is foolish, or both. Marriage is not an overwhelming reason. I advise my unmarried female friends to stick with the names they have, or if they wish to change for some good reason (e.g., they consider their given names to be socially or psychologically unacceptable), to choose their own names, not to accept someone else's identity.

Absolutely yes! It seems very absurd to me for someone to drop her name upon marriage. It is a reflection of old ideas and old standards to give up your name; when women became possessions of their husbands at marriage it was logical to take their names. I think the custom is rather barbaric, frankly. I would even go so far as to say that it should be illegal to give up your birth name, because as long as women do it, that same attitude of men possessing women will prevail. Why not stop it now, so that people can start reevaluating the principle behind it?

Oh, yes. It really annoys me that my girlfriend got married and went out and bought monogrammed everythings to show off her matrimonial state. She made a production of her charge cards: to the salesperson she'd say, "The name I'm signing here is not the name on the card ... here's my driver's license ... you see, I just got married." ...*ad nauseam*. Her assertion was clear: "I am *now* a complete woman — I snared me a man." She could have been the president of GM and she would not have shown her face in public until she got a ring on her finger. *It sickens me.*

Well, I suppose I do think that women should be encouraged to keep their names.... If women give up their names to their husbands, their identities go, too, it seems to me. Their job security will come second, their income will be figured in as offsetting the cost of the babysitter and the TV dinner, or as "a little job to keep her out of Bloomingdale's" (this is a quotation from an acquaintance of my father). A woman announces by taking her husband's name that she is not averse to being assumed to be an eventual housewife and mother as her paramount duties, with social responsibilities as "Mrs. John Doe" thrown in.

Other women, less emphatic than those quoted above, also stated that they would encourage women to keep their own names after marriage. Their more moderate statements ranged from reasons of identity to purely practical considerations:

For a number of reasons, my response is "yes." First, as a devoted amateur family genealogist, I have often been frustrated in trying to trace female lines of the family because the women seemed to drift into married anonymity upon marriage. Second, I see that marriage can, indeed, tend to submerge the identity of one partner over the other. I think that a couple should use a hyphenated version of both names or should select a third name upon marriage — or each should retain his/her own name and provide children with another surname.

A woman should maintain her own name or hyphenate it with her husband's name, especially if she is well-known in her own right — Jane Goodall or Janet Taylor Spence, for example. Otherwise, people should call themselves whatever they feel best expresses the way they feel about themselves. . . . Also, I think that a new name can be symbolic for an escape from an unhappy past or event. Your name is a very personal thing.

Yes. So many women have to make most of the concessions in a relationship, which I don't feel is fair.

I think that women should be encouraged to keep their birth-given surnames forever. A name carries with it associations of a lifetime, of a certain psyche, which is a particular human being. Marriage is a union of two separate entities — not a merger of personalities. In order for a woman to remain autonomous, she must retain her name.

A few women advocated the retention of birth names, but expressed concern that they would then only be perpetuating their fathers' names:

I'm still very troubled that it's only my father's name I carry.

Although keeping one's surname is keeping a patrilineal name, it still maintains heritage and family meaning. Eventually, future generations will be able to associate their families with two names, two histories, two unique lives — one from their mothers, one from their fathers.

"It's a Personal Choice." Even more of the women who responded to the questionnaire felt that a name is a matter of individual choice. They maintained that each person should simply be allowed to decide what is right for her.

I would encourage freedom of choice. I don't particularly care if other women feel more comfortable with their husbands' names, but I don't want to insist everyone keep their names (maybe they don't like them — the only reason I can see for giving them up). Social pressure works against retaining one's maiden name, so I suppose the existence of choice should be emphasized.

Women should be left free to make a choice. If society started "encouraging" women to do one or the other, a lot of women would once again not be making a choice. They would only follow along with what everyone else was doing. A woman should make a choice that she is comfortable with. Most of the decision will be based on whatever self-pride was instilled from her family — whether she knows it or not. All we can do is be tolerant.

"Let a thousand flowers bloom," says Mao. Let everyone pick whatever name they like. I don't think it ought to be an issue, and I don't think what anyone calls himself or herself is anyone's business but his/her own — unless an attempt at fraud is there. Encourage or discourage a woman to keep or change her name? Why bother? Let her decide.

Well, I think women should be encouraged to use the name they feel comfortable with. I'm a little too conservative to countenance the practice of choosing wholly new names. After all, I guess a name is more than an assigned number. It has some history and significance.

Several emphasized that women ought to be made aware of the options available to them in keeping or choosing a name. Many women, they pointed out, think that they *must* change to their husbands' names.

Most women, even younger ones, fail to recognize that they have a choice, unless they have an example in the form of someone they know. When it comes to keeping your own name, it really seems to make a difference if you have friends who have kept their names.

I think that women should have complete freedom of choice over their names. Along with the choice, women should have easily accessible information regarding the process of name-changing and the possible ramifications.

Women should be told they have a choice, then decide for themselves. So many women ask me how I got to keep my name. They don't know the alternatives when they get married, and after they change their names it is more involved to get their old names back (lawyers, court) and certainly more expensive.

A small percentage hesitated to recommend keeping one's name or had no opinion either way:

As for encouraging women to keep their surnames, I don't know. Things are in flux now, and I wouldn't presume to know which is better in the long run. I can just follow my own instinct about what's right for me right now, but as for society over time, I don't have any idea.

I'm not as radical as I was ten years ago. Then I thought that no woman should change her name. Now I think that there are women who use their husbands' names and also have good relationships. I do, however, think that a person's name is very important and I'm glad I've kept mine.

I don't think it should be an issue. Some women very much want to change their names, and I don't think it should be looked on as bad, especially if these women have no career ambitions.

No! Some women are happy to change their names; none of us should be made to feel that what we are doing is somehow wrong. [This woman took her husbands' surnames in her first two marriages, then regained her birth name and has continued to use it since she has remarried.]

After I had read all the strong feelings, opinions, and recommendations offered by the women in the study, I found Lania Groleau's advice refreshing:

Women, and men, should do whatever they want to with their own names — it is convenient to keep your own name sometimes, it is nice to share someone else's name sometimes, or you can express your own personality and creativity by choosing your own name. The only thing is to have a name that means something to you personally, one that you've thought about a bit.

7. "But What Does Your Husband Think?"

My husband has always been supportive about my keeping my own name. It now represents an outward example of our attitudes toward marriage and feminism.

My husband wasn't thrilled—he was particularly concerned about family identity and the children (then non-existent). Over time, he has realized what a non-issue names are and I haven't heard anything negative from him.

My husband hated it—he worried about what "other people" would think.

When a married woman uses her birth name or adopts a name of her own choosing, her husband (or husband-to-be) may react with applause, outrage, or yawns. Three-quarters of the women in the survey were married, and I asked these women and their husbands how the men feel—not only about their wives having different names, but about the implications. In addition, I asked them what impact, if any, the name issue has had upon their marriages. To get a different viewpoint, I also questioned a small number of married men whose wives had taken the husbands' surnames.

Reactions from Husbands in Two-Name Families

Most married men whom I surveyed had either positive or neutral attitudes about the fact that their wives had kept their birth names or had taken hyphenated names. Few were actively opposed to the idea.

Some men felt good about their wives' decision from the start. Curtis Schneider said simply, "It was fine with me. I didn't want to change my name. Why should she?" Another man declared, "I'm proud to be a part of a decision on Jane's part to maintain her own identity. It's a subtle hint that we are not possessions of each other. I cringe when I see a grown woman allow herself to be called 'Mrs. Thomas Smith,' etc." George Lott, who married his wife (now deceased) when both were in their forties, wrote, "I enjoyed Annemarie's using her name; I like independent women, and this was one aspect of showing her independence. I may have had some special macho appreciation of her retaining her surname: it gave me a feeling of greater worth for myself, as I was secure enough to let her retain her name."

Some men even encouraged their wives or wives-to-be to keep their birth names. Cathy Stone Wilson had planned to take her husband's surname after they married. But he suggested that she use both their surnames — Stone and Wilson. She said, "My husband has been very supportive about my name. He always takes care to introduce me with my full name, calling attention to the difference. When we go to civic functions (which we do a great deal because of our jobs), he always makes reservations in our two names to enhance the chances of getting a name tag that is correct."

Wilma Weichinger, a Chicago banker, wrote: "My husband said it was my decision — but he did talk to women in his law firm to see if they were glad they had changed their names. He really researched the topic and was supportive when I decided to keep my name. He always introduces me and says he didn't change his name when we got married."

Wilma's sister Judith, who is a minister, also had a positive experience with her husband. "Before I was married, when I was making up my mind what to do, I literally did not know what my husband-to-be wanted me to do. He said it was my name and my decision. Only after my decision did I find out he hoped I'd keep my surname. He has had some comments from people about why he didn't have more control over me, etc. (questioning his 'masculinity'), but he can and does tell them off at that point!"

Alice Jermyn took her stepfather's surname when she married for the second time. She wrote this about her husband's reaction: "Jerry fully supported me in my choice. He recognizes, respects and loves the fact that I am an independent woman. He realizes that he has more than a wife; he has a partner, and he would not want it any other way. And after all, he is glad that I did not choose to keep my first husband's name."

Other women also mentioned that their husbands immediately accepted and agreed with their decisions:

> My husband was supportive; he asked me whether I would keep my name only moments after asking me to marry him. He has never expressed anything other than satisfaction with my choice.

> My husband always supported my right to use my own name. He discouraged me from using his name, and he was right. I felt wrong with his name and changed back to my birth name.

However, it was unusual for husbands to have an immediate and unquestioning acceptance of their wives' names. Many felt an initial ambivalence or even opposition to the idea, but gradually came to accept and support it. They felt at first that their wives were showing a lack of love or a lack of commitment to the marriage by not changing their names, and worried that it might harm their relationships. After the women explained their reasons to their husbands and the men had time to adjust to the idea, they felt more comfortable with it. David Nussbaum, a 29-year-old graduate student in clinical psychology, expressed his feelings in psychoanalytic terms:

> I personalized her decision and was hurt by it, i.e., she didn't think my name was good enough or didn't like its awkward sound. I felt like it was a rejection of me, not only my name.... Now I feel entirely different. I recognize her need to retain her identity and roots and have separated her desire to keep her name from her feelings toward me. I consider it as a matter of course and actively encourage all independent movement such as this.... For a change that I initially considered so threatening, I must say that it has evolved into something very positive for each of us.

Joseph Mitchell, a 32-year-old physician, wrote, "At first I felt anger and hurt. I wanted Lucy to assume my name because of my pride in my family and its heritage. I feel much better now. It was simply a matter of viewing things from her perspective — i.e., wanting to preserve her identity and her family connection."

His wife said much the same thing: "He felt initially hurt, but realized he would not change his own name, and therefore understood."

A large number of women reported similar reactions from their husbands. As June Hobarth said, "Initially my husband-to-be was taken aback. Letting his traditional background get in the way of logical thinking, he was wondering why I had, in effect, rejected him. When he realized that it was not he who was rejected, but rather his name, he was proud that his wife-to-be had the desire to remain her own person."

"My husband was a little put off at first," wrote Margaret Gunnison, "as I think he felt it was an affront to his name and in some way implied a lack of love and respect. That quickly passed when I explained my reasons of 'self identity' and he is now quite supportive of women retaining their maiden names upon marriage."

Some men, fewer than 20 percent, remained ambivalent about the idea. They respected their wives' wishes, but actually would have liked the women to change their surnames. Yvette Hollar explained, "My husband was mildly disappointed — not because his family name was so important to him that he wanted to perpetuate it, but because he felt it was a sign of commitment to him that I wasn't making. He also admitted that his masculinity, his sense of power and authority, was somewhat damaged. But he realized I felt much more strongly about it than he did, so he didn't object much."

Several other women said that their husbands were bothered when they did not change their names, and this was confirmed by the men. Edward Richmond said, "I was surprised and upset to a small degree. I would have preferred that she use the same name. But it was her name and not mine, so it was her decision." Arnold Jamieson had similar feelings: "I guess there was a part of me which hoped she would take my name, but it was neither a strong nor a controlling feeling. I felt that it was her decision and that I would support any decision she made."

Only a small minority, about 3 to 4 percent, of the men involved in the survey (those surveyed directly or those whose wives were surveyed) had strong negative attitudes about their wives' nominal choices. Peggy Reiner said, "My husband was miffed, insulted, felt it reflected my mistrust of him." Other women wrote:

> My husband dislikes it and socially refers to me with his last name.

> My husband does not like my use of my maiden name. Because of this and also because I do identify with my marital relationship and how we relate together to the outside world, I have taken his surname for all else but work.

"But What Does Your Husband Think?"

The men who were surveyed expressed themselves more cautiously. Ralph Rooker said, "My life exposure was such that I believed a wife took her husband's last name as a natural course of marriage." Richard Alleyn said, "For recordkeeping and financial joint accounts, it's a pain in the neck. Personally, it's a minor inconvenience." Aaron Golden maintained that he really didn't care about his wife's name and was just "impatient with the confusion and extra paperwork and explanations we have to live with daily." However, he was more candid when he added, "The breaking of 'social order' (from the mechanical point of view) and thousands of years of tradition better be truly worth it to you gals!"

Anne Decker and her husband were an extreme case. She indicated that the name issue was "a major hassle" with her husband from the beginning. "I was adamant," she wrote, "and refused to get married if my fiance forced this point. He refused to marry me unless I made this 'proclamation of love' (read ownership). It was actually a factor that delayed our marriage. . . ." When they finally married, Anne did keep her birth name. At the time that she participated in the survey, she and her husband had separated. She wrote that "my husband looked at my responses to your questionnaire and stated that my choice to retain my name was, in fact, why we were getting a divorce. He said that my 'bossy' attitude had caused him to be an underachiever, which was one of my complaints in asking for a divorce."

It is understandable that most men whose wives keep their own names encourage, accept, or at least tolerate this practice. For one thing, women who decide to keep their own names are not likely to marry extremely traditional or socially conservative men. These men may not always be willing to share half the housework or to feed the baby at 3:00 a.m., but they generally can accept that their wives have some existence outside of being wives.

Although some men reacted negatively at first to the idea of a woman keeping her name, most said that they subsequently realized how important it was to their wives. They recognized, at least in a general way, the implications of a woman keeping her name: her desire to maintain a separate identity and some sense of independence. Furthermore, most of the men in the survey were highly educated professionals. While education does not magically erase sexist prejudices, it may help to give men a less stereotypical view of women and to bring them into contact with women who are well-educated and often independent.

Impact Upon Marriages

The great majority of the husbands and wives in the survey thought that the women's name choices had either a positive impact on their marriages or none at all. If these couples had clashed badly over the choice of a name, they probably either would not have married, or the women would have taken their husbands' names.

Some couples considered their marriages had been strengthened when the women maintained their own names. Both husbands and wives believed the women's increased self-esteem and self-confidence benefited the overall relationships. Gregory Rhodes said, "it symbolizes the fact that Susan is not, as it were, a subset of me, which probably helps maintain that feeling between us." Another man observed that because his wife uses a different name than his, she does not feel "owned." "I think it has helped my marriage to be healthier," wrote Aimee Marshall, "mostly because it has helped me to be more sure of myself as an individual."

Just the fact that a couple had to confront the question of names sometimes had a beneficial effect on their relationship because it encouraged them to communicate more. Deborah Wein said that this was the case with her and her husband: "The fact that I kept my name brought my husband and me to very open, continual, and, in the beginning, constant discussion about the meaning and operationalization of an egalitarian marriage. The change over the years, and the growth, has been tremendous." Ellen Edwards, whose husband does not like the fact that she has kept her name, said that "your questionnaire was a good basis for Ralph and me to discuss this issue — we aren't any closer to agreement, but perhaps closer in understanding."

For all the couples who said that the name issue had a positive impact upon their marriages, there was an approximately equal number who said that it had no impact. As one woman observed, "A name hardly affects a love relationship." Most felt that it simply wasn't an issue anymore, if it had ever been. Among these couples, the women felt good about having their own names, and the men generally accepted it.

Many couples in the study made it clear that they highly value independence and separateness in their marriages; to them this is simply an acknowledgement that both a husband and wife are individuals. They want to preserve this individuality within the marriage, as well as build a committed relationship with common goals. William Adelman feels that he and his wife using different surnames "has enabled each of us to maintain separate identities while concomitantly being known as a couple who feels strongly about marriage as a commitment." After observing that using her own name had a positive impact on her marriage, Ronna Sollmer wrote, "it's indicative rather than influential. I think it is part and parcel of keeping our separate professional interests, hobbies, and identities. We haven't tried to merge into one whole; each of us is a whole person, not half a person."

Reactions from Husbands in Shared-Name Families

When I questioned married men whose wives shared their surnames, these men said they were pleased with the arrangement. In fact, most said they would not have liked it any other way. "If my wife had suggested that she not take my surname," wrote a scientist, "I probably would have been insulted." A physician said, "I would have responded negatively. Even though I realize that for many women changing their name is inconvenient, to me it seems almost like couples aren't 'really married' when they don't share a family name." Another man said, "Women keeping their maiden names doesn't bother me as long as I don't have to deal with it in my own personal situation." All three of these men are in their early thirties and are well-educated professionals, similar to many of the men I surveyed whose wives had kept their own names.

A few of these husbands were not quite so traditional. A 39-year-old financial analyst wrote, "My wife wanted to take my name. I don't believe that it would have bothered me if she would have continued to use her maiden name." Other men wrote:

If a woman wants to keep her name, that's fine.

If my wife had wanted to keep her maiden name, I would have fully respected her option and accepted her break with the traditional procedure. Sometimes it's very important to a woman to keep her name, especially if she's older and has established a professional reputation with her maiden name. Women deserve the right, equally with men, to have LARGE EGOS reflected in usage of names! [The man who wrote this is 53.]

69

It is no surprise that when people make a particular decision, they tend to support and justify it. The married men whom I surveyed—those who shared a surname with their wives and those who did not—defended the choices they had made. The men whose wives had used their birth names or hyphenated names came to accept and often to approve of their wives' choices. On the other hand, the men whose wives had taken the husbands' surnames generally believed that *this* was the right and proper course of action.

8. "But What Will the Neighbors Think?"

When a married woman decides to retain her birth name, hyphenate her name, or make some other alteration in her name, her husband's feelings will probably have the most impact upon her. But the opinions of other relatives, particularly parents, can also be important. Unless a woman is completely alienated from or indifferent to her parents, it can be painful to have them vehemently opposed to a decision that is significant to her. Even if this happens, there are things that she can do to make it easier for both her and her parents.

Some women do face very vigorous opposition from their families. Kit Carlson said, "My parents blew their cork. We must have spent $50 each on long-distance phone calls arguing about it. My parents tried every dirty guilt trip in the book to get me to change my mind."

Other women reported equally strong reactions:

> Both of our parents were shocked and considered it either impossible or a whim. I still think they don't consider it legal or permanent!

> My family (including aunts, uncles, grandparents) were totally appalled, questioned whether it was legal, questioned whether we were really married, and implied I would probably go to hell as a result.

> My family was very upset and tried to talk me out of it—they were afraid people wouldn't know we were married and would think we were "living in sin." (Even today, seven years after my marriage, some members of my family refuse to use my chosen name.)

Two women who took family surnames from grandparents haven't even told their parents. "My mother and father live across the country," Carrie Revelle wrote. "I haven't dared tell them, as I expect their reaction to be very negative: my father hurt and my mother giving ridicule." Joanne Bischler said, "I changed my name a year and a half

71

ago and still haven't told my parents. Maybe this winter. They'll have a fit."

In other cases, parents just regarded their daughters' actions as strange. One woman said, "My parents thought it another bizarre action in an already bizarre life," while another said, "They were understanding but probably thought I was flaky."

Some parents worried that their daughters' retention of their birth names was a harbinger of doom for their marriages. "My parents were concerned that it meant I didn't have much faith in my marriage," wrote Leigh Derman-Stender. Marge McGhill's family thought she wasn't "being loyal or a real wife."

On the other hand, some parents were pleased. "My parents didn't bat an eyelid," wrote Barbara Berg. "I'm sure they always knew I felt this way, and supported it." Marie Dupree said, "I think my parents were pleased — especially my father. We have a very small immediate family and in one sense (as there are no sons) I am continuing the family name (my father's, that is)." It took Anita Calabrese's parents a while to accept her decision: "At first my parents were embarrassed and almost appalled. Now, seven years later, they're proud and tell all their friends about the choice I made."

Norma Goodwin Veridan asked her parents, then 77 and 79, what they thought of her new surname, which was a combination of their first names: "My father said, 'At first I thought it was a little strange, but when I understood why you wanted to do it and what it means, I think it's fine.' My mother said, 'When you explained it, I was (pause — almost shyly) honored.'"

Mothers

It appears that mothers feel more strongly than fathers do when daughters don't take their husbands' names. Generally their objections are on the grounds of convention: "What will people think?" or, "How will we introduce you?" or, "How should we address mail to you?" But I think that their reasons are more profound.

To many parents, especially mothers, it is important that their daughters marry; in a certain sense, perhaps they see it as a measure of their success as parents. Wearing a husband's name is an "advertisement" of marriage, and when a woman decides not to take her husband's name, her mother is often upset. Margaret Thomas said, "My mother was shocked. Her immediate reaction was, 'But how will we write it up in the newspaper?'" Eva Dolan wrote that even though she's been married for six years, "My mother is still convinced that the mail carrier thinks we are having an affair!" Nina Cavelli, who took back her birth name after she was divorced, said, "My mother was horrified that I would give up the social status of being a 'Mrs.,' and said that returning to my maiden name implied to the world that no man had wanted me."

Virginia Benz explained her mother's reaction slightly differently. Her explanation says as much about her as it does about her mother: "I detect resentment from my mother at times at my use of my own name. This is part of her general resentment that I have 'fought' for my own way in life, rather than letting my husband's choices determine my adult life. I fully understand this attitude of hers."

The strength of feeling that some mothers had about their daughters' names was striking. (Of course, the women who had "horror stories" to tell about their mothers tended to go into more detail than those whose mothers accepted their choices without a lot of drama.) According to the daughters, mothers were "upset," "fought it bitterly," "felt resentment," and so on. One woman wrote, "My mother went up to guests at our wedding, exclaiming in shock and outrage about 'what I had done.'" Judith Weichinger's mother, a conservative Southern woman, reacted unusually strongly:

> My mother went nuts! She didn't speak to me (literally) the first two months we were married. Then she continued to write to me as Mrs. Ron Alton for about one or two years until we had it out again. She saw it as a total rejection of everything she stood for. It was a very rough road with her. Occasionally she slips up now (five and a half years later), but usually she respects it. . . . It's one area where I obviously cut the apron strings and she didn't like it.

Wilma Weichinger, Judith's sister, married a few years later and kept her birth name, too. Wilma said that her mother's reaction wasn't quite as bad "since it was the second time. She still writes me as Mrs. Husband's Name and I don't make a big deal about it."

Fortunately, most mothers, even Judith's and Wilma's, eventually come to accept their daughters' names, even thought they still may be bothered by the idea. Some feel it is useless to continue to object.

Martha Holmes Davis said, "my mother fought it bitterly for about six months, then gave in, hoping I'd come to my senses eventually."

Other mothers decide that it is not so bad after all. "Although my mother tried to talk me out of it," wrote Carrie Grafton, "six months after I was married she said she had changed her mind and was proud that I had chosen to keep my name. She was impressed by the fact that I had wanted to keep my present middle name (which is her maiden name). That would not have been possible had I taken my husband's surname because in the South a woman traditionally takes her maiden name as her middle name upon marriage."

About a third of the women who mentioned their mothers' attitudes said that the mothers reacted favorably to their daughters' choice of name. Amy Kelly, for example, wrote, "My mother has had her 'consciousness raised' with respect to feminism and staunchly defends my decision to her friends!"

Abigail K. Alcott, who adopted her great-grandmother's surname after changing her name in three marriages, got a gratifying response from her mother. She wrote: "The best part was when I told my mother. I said I was thinking of changing my name and I wanted to try it out on her. The name I chose was her grandmother's. She said, 'Oh, that's beautiful,' and cried! That's when I knew I had chosen the right name."

Fathers

When a woman keeps her birth name, her father is generally less bothered by it than her mother. Melissa Jane Brown said, "My mother's first reaction was that 'it will kill your father' until she heard him say that he didn't think it was a bad idea!" Many fathers were glad that their daughters had kept the family name. A. June McDonald wrote, "Actually I think my father, who is very conservative, was rather pleased. Neither he nor his brother has any sons, so this way I could carry his name along a little longer." Nina Cavelli said that her father was very proud of his family surname and was pleased that she decided to bear this name again after her divorce.

There were some fathers who flatly disapproved of their daughters' choices. Like a lot of the mothers, they worried that other people would think their daughters were not married and were "living in sin." Rae

Carter wrote, "My father said our names on the mailbox made it look like we were 'shacked up together.'"

Then there were those who needed some time to adjust to the idea:

> When we announced our engagement, my father said *he* would never marry a woman who wouldn't change her name (a rather irrelevant observation in view of the facts!). He has, however, respected my choice.

> My father expressed fear that people would think we were just living together. At first he said he would refuse to continue using my name when he wrote. He very quickly seemed to adjust and now readily accepts my choice. I think this was helped by my absolute certainty about what I was doing.

> My *very* traditional parents at first looked askance. Later, my father particularly was thrilled when my name appeared publicly a great deal.

In-Laws

The questionnaire results indicate that a woman's in-laws are often upset when she uses her birth name. In fact, almost all of the women who mentioned their in-laws' reactions said that they were negative. Susan Novak, who has been married for 10 years, wrote, "My husband's parents often still refuse to recognize I do not have their name. It continues to be an issue with them." Another woman observed, "My mother-in-law still won't accept the situation. She recently informed my husband that I should stop this nonsense because 'nobody is doing that anymore. That's out of style.'"

Barbara Knopf said: "His parents resented it deeply. While we were engaged, he lent me $100. When his mother found out, she said 'She's willing to take your money, but not your name.' In all fairness, their daughter Barbara died at age 12, and they wanted another 'Barbara Greer.'"

Some women hesitated to tell their in-laws at all. "My mother-in-law doesn't know I kept my birth name," Wilma Weichinger wrote. "She thinks it's *awful* (she told me before we got married), so we just didn't tell her." Kathryn Hindon said, "My husband's family don't know — they would go ape! I don't see a reason to upset them unnecessarily; they don't care for me much, anyway."

In some cases, in-laws interpret it as a slight to them or to their name. As Debra Gross explained, "My father-in-law took it as a direct insult to his revered family name." Quite often they are afraid that their daughter-in-law is showing a lack of commitment to her marriage. Joan Jeffrey-Norton said, "my mother-in-law was very concerned that I really didn't want to be married to her son." Another woman wrote:

> My husband's father, who is usually a very reasonable man, was particularly distressed. He felt that my not changing my name was a sign of not being completely committed to the marriage. (This was after my husband and I had been 'dating' for five years; my future father-in-law knew me quite well.)

Most in-laws, however, did not feel as strongly as Susan Goldsmith's. They threatened to paint over her name and her husband's on their apartment door!

Jane Shapiro, a university professor, wrote that the problems she expected with her in-laws never came to pass:

> Even though my husband wanted me to keep my maiden name, I expected problems with his family. (He is the oldest of ten children in what I have always seen as a traditional family.) But the problems never materialized and I attribute this to my husband's attitude. He is tolerant with those who are not comfortable with our decision, firm with those who are being reactionary, and humorous with everyone else. When his mother suggested people might think we were living in sin, he just looked at her with the cutest smile.

Grandparents

Parents may hit the roof. In-laws may be upset. Grandparents, on the whole, approve or don't care. They're a bit farther away emotionally from the situation, have a better perspective on it, and perhaps have lived long enough to see that it's not an earthshaking issue. "My husband's grandmothers, who were 'spared' the news for as long as possible, were not even mildly shocked," wrote Nancy Merton. "One grandmother's only response was 'so what?'" Charlotte B. Walker, who took back her birth name after divorce, said, "My grandmother thought it was 'great.' Does that tell you something about my grandmother?"

Some women mentioned that their grandparents didn't understand that the granddaughters had kept their names, and therefore addressed mail to them as Mr. and Mrs. "My grandparents never really caught on. They know, but they forget," wrote one woman.

Siblings

Only a small number (12 percent) of the women in my study reported the reactions of their siblings. The majority of siblings approved of their sisters' birth name retention, name changes, or whatever. There were still a substantial number, though, who were ambivalent or opposed to their sisters' actions. Marjorie Townsend wrote:

> Oddly, my siblings object strongly, feeling it is "normal" to change names when one marries and that we are making life very difficult for everyone by forcing them to remember two names! There have been no philosophical arguments on the subject; just the mundane ones of "how do you address a wedding invitation?"

Some sisters had underlying reasons for their opposition:

> One of my sisters was quite upset because she had wanted to keep her own name and her husband was adamantly opposed. Because of her profession, her credibility, and her prominence in her field, she wanted to maintain that personal identity. Now that she and her husband are separated, she's talking about taking back her birth name.

> I think that my older sister, who has a more traditional marriage, felt threatened and for years used my husband's name when addressing mail to me.

In some families, brothers and sisters differed in their opinions. Lin Ott said, "One brother was supportive, one brother non-committal, and one brother still addresses mail to me under my married name." Thea Harmon's sisters ran the gamut: "One didn't care, one thought it was a good thing, one disapproved, one was confused and uses both names."

Friends

The majority of women reported that their friends supported their choice of name. After Sara Willard divorced and took back her birth name, she said, "Most of my friends expressed delight. Several said that I provided an excellent example and they wished they had never taken their husbands' surnames." Marni Politte Harmony, who chose a new surname with her husband, Peter, wrote that her friends "thought it was fine — they were delighted. Most expressed the wish that they had considered such an option."

Some women's friends approved of their decisions, but did not emulate them:

> The friends who really counted in my life thought I was gutsy, and respected my decision, although *none of them* retained their birth names upon marriage.

> They tell me what a good idea I had after they've had to wait in line two hours to get driver's licenses changed when they get married. And they tell me about the hassles of changing names back after a divorce. Yet *every one* of them continues to change her name with successive marriages. Fools!

About a quarter of the women that I surveyed said that they got mixed reactions. Nancy Garvin, who took back her birth name after 13 years of marriage, said of her friends: "About half were pro, half con, no in-between. Some thought Bill and I were near divorce, others didn't understand why he would support it, and some didn't think it was legal. But my closest friends were understanding and thought it was neat."

Judith Weichinger said that some friends thought her decision was strange, but they respected it. "Many of these friends," she observed, "now are smothering under their husbands or divorced and taking back their names. They see it differently than they did five years ago."

Norma Goodwin Veridan observed that her friends' reactions were distributed along gender lines:

> Most of my women friends understood the process I went through and many were supportive, even those who would not themselves consider such a change. Many of the men I talked with, even those I had thought quite understanding of women's concerns, didn't understand why I would want to do it. It seems to me that people who have never

78

experienced changing their names find it difficult to understand one
who chooses to change without benefit of tradition.

Some friends were just confused. Rachel Crandall, who lives in
Columbia, South Carolina, said, "At least one still thinks that David
had to change his name to Crandall if I didn't change mine — hence mail
to Mr. and Mrs. David Crandall."

Some friends felt that the subject was not even worth commenting
upon. This seems to have been most often true for women who live in
large urban areas or in academic communities. Ellen Eisenstadt, who
lives in the Boston area, wrote, "It was discussed a number of years ago
and is now considered simply a matter of personal preference among
my social group." She added, "My husband has one friend who expressed
his preference that his wife take his name. Others who share that senti-
ment may simply not express it to us, because they don't want to appear
socially or politically backward."

Michelle La Grande lives in San Diego. When she took back her
birth name after divorce, she reported no strong responses from her
friends. "After all," she said, "this is California!" Daphne Ellis, another
Californian, said, "The community I lived in before I separated from
my husband was highly unorthodox. Name changes — religious, social,
political, or otherwise — were so common we all had to take notes."

Andrea Bell, who is a graduate student, said, "I got no particular
reaction. In an academic setting, where I am, it's common for a woman
to keep her name." Even in academe, though, one can meet with some
disapproval. Caroline Lang reported that "some older faculty friends
sighed and commented on how hard it is to remember the names of
couples with two last names. We are often referred to as the Barnes-
Lang unit, or Barnes-Lang, Inc."

Very few women (fewer than 2 percent of those who responded to
the question) felt that their friends opposed their choice of a name.
Diane Hollins was unusual in writing, "I am disappointed in how many
friends think what I did was both odd and an insult to my husband.
Many ask if I had Craig's 'permission' before doing what I did."

Among Rebecca Harris' friends, the important issue was not that
she kept her own name. "The biggest reaction," she wrote, "was rather
to the fact of Eddie and me getting married. We were somewhat legend-
ary for staying together for about six years before deciding to tie the
knot!"

79

Attitude

If a woman's parents, in-laws, or friends have some difficulty with her choice of names, her attitude is clearly important in keeping friction to a minimum. Many relatives do not intend a personal insult when they don't use the correct name. Perhaps they live in a small town or rural area where people tend to be conservative in their social mores, or perhaps they are older people, such as grandparents, who may not understand the woman's wishes.

Some women took an understanding attitude with their relatives. Marie Dupree, who uses her birth name, said, "My husband's parents and relatives refer to me as Mrs. Cambridge, but I told them to call me whatever was comfortable for them. They come from a small conservative town (they were dairy farmers), while my parents were military, well-travelled and educated."

When Jane Patton kept her name at marriage, her mother would not recognize this. "My mother is a traditional woman," she wrote. "She addresses all mail to 'Mrs. Edward Tischler,' rather than to 'Ms. Jane Patton.' We get along very well so I do not push the issue although I have requested she not do it."

H. Jane Walken, a physician, wrote that at first her family and in-laws were unsure how to address her and her husband, "but everyone relaxed when they realized I wouldn't be offended to be 'Mrs. Price' at times and wouldn't be upset if it wasn't done just as I wished."

Another woman, a lawyer, was matter-of-fact, but considerate, with her in-laws:

> My husband's family sometimes still introduce me as Mrs. Peel. I don't make a big deal of it with his relatives because I don't want to hurt their feelings. If I introduce myself I use my maiden name and explain who I am. His parents asked me recently how they should introduce me. I said I hadn't changed my name, and they should use my maiden name. If they felt uncomfortable with that, I said, they could use the excuse that since I am a professional, I kept my maiden name for business purposes.

On the other hand, Barbara Knopf wrote, "Some of my family insists on using Knopf-Greer or Greer [her husband's name] as my name – not just older people, either. When they send me mail like that,

I've been returning it as 'Addressee unknown.'" By doing this, Barbara demonstrates her convictions dramatically, but she also antagonizes a lot of relatives.

Responses to the survey suggest that families are happiest when women try to be flexible and understanding with relatives who may be hostile, very traditional, or just confused. Women may find this difficult at times, particularly when people won't even try to see their point of view. Sometimes, though, it may come down to a choice between ideological purity and familial dissension.

9. Naming the Children

After a woman marries, decides on the name she wants to use, and trains her family and friends, she may think that her name problems are over. However, if she and her husband have a child, a new dilemma is born. Should the child have Daddy's surname, Mommy's surname, a combination, or a completely new surname?

The decision about what surname to give one's children is an individual one. Each couple must answer a few questions for themselves. How important is it to the father that his name be continued by his children? For a woman who has kept her own name, is it important to her that she perpetuate her name beyond her own generation, or is it enough that she keep the same name all her life? How will the children be affected by their surname, particularly if it is a hyphenated one, or one that is different from that of both parents?

I found that women who have kept their own names are very concerned about the issue of children's names. Claire Devlin said, "The retention of my birth name caused few problems by itself. The big crisis came with how to name the children." Many women who already have children discussed this question at length with their husbands, but are still ambivalent about their choice, particularly if they gave the children the father's surname. Some question the utility of a woman keeping her own name if that name is not carried on into the next generation.

Women who have not yet had children see the problem, too. Rivka Greenberg, for example, wrote:

> I think it's very important for women to have the power to name their children. My husband and I have talked about giving some of our children his name and some mine. I am not concerned about problems of family cohesion which some people have raised. Hopefully, I'll be able to feel that there's some resolution of my feelings before we actually have children. The idea of a woman's lineage in families appeals to me greatly, but I also want any daughter, or son, I have to be fully

autonomous from both my husband and me when they grow up, at least as far as that's humanly possible.

Other women had similar concerns:

I think the major problem with names is not so much whether to keep your own or not, but what to name children. Should all family members have different names? I haven't had to face this one yet, but I must say that I don't know what I'd do.

We have considered adopting and have not quite decided what to do. Hyphenating the two names is awkward. My husband leans toward my name as the simpler. I'm not sure — thinking that both of us should be represented.

I discovered that the husbands of women who have kept their own names are not terribly interested in the question of children's names. Perhaps this is so because the children will bear the fathers' names unless the parents decide otherwise. Slightly fewer than half the men surveyed said that in a family in which the parents use different surnames, the children should be given the father's surname. Most used as their rationale either tradition (one man wrote, "this is a patrilineal society") or simplicity for the sake of the child. As Thomas Carver said, "I still hold to some tradition, but my reasons are for the sake of the child. I feel that generally children can be quite stigmatized by name selection, both given and surname. Growing up nowadays is hard enough as it is without adding an additional identity problem to it." Another man was honest enough to write, "Ego also comes into this. I would like my children to carry my name."

About 25 percent of the men said that children should be given a combination surname, and about another 25 percent didn't know or hadn't decided. Only one man wanted his children to bear their mother's surname because, he said, "It is a prettier name than mine." It is important to note that many of the men who advocated combination surnames or other more unusual solutions are not yet fathers. They may feel differently when faced with the reality of naming their own children.

How, in fact, did the women in my study choose to name their children? Of those who have children, the great majority (84.5 percent) gave their children the father's surname. (Ten percent of these also used the mother's surname as a middle name.) They gave several different reasons for this choice.

Aurora Figueroa said that her son had his father's surname rather than a hyphenated name "because my husband has a long Polish name, and together with my name it would be too awkward for a child. Why his name and not mine? I'm not sure." Several women agreed that hyphenated names for children are too cumbersome.

Others explained that their husbands wanted to carry on their surnames. Susan Garvin wrote: "My husband is an only child so we wanted to keep the name alive; I, on the other hand, have brothers to keep my family's surname going." (It is interesting that many of us perceive that a name does not just identify a family, but embodies it; when the name dies, the family dies.)

Many women gave children the father's name because they felt no compelling reason to use any other. I fall into this category myself. It wasn't particularly important to me that my surname be kept alive, and my husband's surname (Adams) is easily pronounced and spelled, so it seemed like a good choice. We even decided that if we had a boy (we did) we would go the whole patrilineal route and name him after his father: Richard David Adams III!

Sharon Lebell, in *Naming Ourselves, Naming Our Children*, asserts:

> Women who keep their names, but give their children their husband's last name are cast into the odd position of being symbolically in exile from the rest of their family.... This maternal exile is a dramatic symbolic distortion of the facts of family life.... The truth about family life is that the woman is the central figure and the man is the more remote parent. So in fact, the mother is at the center; yet nominally, she is cast to the periphery.[1]

None of the women in my study mentioned any perception of this "exile." A few were ambivalent about giving their children the father's surname because they thought there must be a more equitable way of showing familial relationships. Others didn't like the minor annoyances of explaining why their names are not the same as their children's. No one, however, mentioned feeling any sense of distance or alienation from her family.

Several couples decided to let gender determine a child's surname: father's name if a boy, mother's name if a girl. Only one of these couples has had a child so far — it was a boy. The other couples have only made this decision in the abstract.

Of the women surveyed who have children, 10 percent gave their children hyphenated names — generally the mother's surname followed by the father's surname. Though they thought this was the most equitable solution, some women expressed concern that these names were too long and complicated, and that they might present problems for the children in school or when they marry. (Most of the children involved are preschoolers now.) It remains to be seen whether the hyphenated names will remain until the children are grown. Some women reported that despite their efforts, people tend to shorten the hyphenated surnames by dropping the first half (usually the mother's name). Thus, the child ends up with his father's surname, anyway.

Only six women (3.8 percent) gave their own surnames to their children. Virginia Alpin and her husband decided to do this because he already had two children with his surname. Sally Pailolo, whose two small children bear her surname, explained that she liked her unusual Hawaiian name and wanted it to continue through her children. She has no brothers to carry on the name. "It was somewhat arbitrary choosing their last name," Sally wrote, "but the final push for using my surname came from my husband. The children's middle name is his surname. So far my older daughter has had no problems with her name."

Two couples created surnames for their children that were different from that of either parent. When Marc Greenwood and Susan Ransom had children, they rejected the usual choices of using the father's surname or a hyphenated one, and took a syllable from each of their names to form the children's surname: Ranwood. (Susan refers to this as their "family" name, but she and her husband still use their own birth names.)

Marc is not happy with the new surname that he and his wife gave their children. He wrote:

> It breaks the family into name groups and erodes the common sense of identity. It also destroys any sense of intergenerational identity between our children and their various grandparents.... Teachers, dentists, etc. get totally lost as to who belongs to whom and it sounds like we have all been through several divorces or other catastrophes. We are on our first marriage and very proud of that in a culture where the whole marriage/family structure is coming apart at the seams.

Naming the Children

Marc feels that the father's surname should be used for the children because the mother's physical bond with the children is naturally stronger: "Using the man's surname helps to balance the natural bond between mother and child that occurs because of the natal and nursing experience." His wife disagrees. Susan is still pleased with the new surname, and thinks the children ought to be told that their name is their own, and that after age 21 they may keep or change it as they please.

Kass Sheedy and Douglas Morea also chose a "family" name for their children, which they themselves do not use. Their children's surname is Ailanthus. As Kass explained:

> Ailanthus is the scientific name for a common tree, also called tree of heaven. We chose that particular name because of the character of the tree (very tough, one of the first to begin growing in a vacant lot, home of the Chinese silkworm) and because it sounds like a reasonable surname. We were consciously avoiding a name that was "cutesy" like Sunshine or Summer.

She said that they had a great deal of trouble getting correct birth certificates issued for their daughters, but since then have had no problems with "official" acceptance of the children's surname. Kass did, however, have to contend with negative reactions from her family:

> My mother was violently opposed to our choice, but I was never able to clearly understand her reasons; perhaps they were not even clear to her. My family (brother, aunts, cousins) simply refuse to acknowledge the children's name. Cards and letters are usually addressed something like: "Kass Sheedy, Douglas, and children." I don't think they are particularly opposed to the idea — they just don't know what to do with it.

Potential Problems

Most of the women in my study took the conventional route and gave children the father's name, so this caused them no bureaucratic or legal problems. Some, however, did have trouble with the fact that their names were not the same as their children's. The first problem, they found, occurred at the hospital when they had to state their children's names on the birth certificate. Beverly Camp, who lives in

New Orleans, wrote, "I couldn't sign my daughter's birth certificate because I didn't have the same last name. (I'd had surgery and I didn't feel like fighting it.)"

Other women had similar experiences:

> The most trouble my husband and I have had because our names are different was at the hospital when our sons were born. Both times hospital staff (nurses and office) showed disapproval. One son's birth certificate had to be filled out three times and there seemed to be serious doubt that my signature was "legal" enough to allow him to be circumcised. And the hospital staff person in charge of sending announcements to the paper refused to use our different names — so I refused to allow the births announced.

> When I had my first daughter (1976), the hospital person who registered the birth (a city official in Washington D.C.) gave me a hard time. She said, "Someday your daughter will ask if you were really married." One year later when my second daughter was born at the same hospital, there was no hassle.

> The city clerk in Boston is under the misapprehension that people don't use hyphenated names. As I had plenty of Massachusetts identification (including a deed to my house), he was forced to give my children birth certificates with my name on them as I currently use it.

I suspect that these women's experiences were the exception, rather than the rule, since no other mothers mentioned problems of this kind. My own experience in this situation was uneventful. When my son was born in 1984 in Raleigh, North Carolina, no one batted an eye when I indicated his parents' names on the birth certificate as Richard Adams and Susan Kupper.

A friend of mine in Chicago had two children while living with, but not married to, the father. Though she used her birth name, she had no difficulty in giving her sons their father's surname on their birth certificates.

Very few women mentioned other problems with having names that are different from their children's. Some do worry about it, though. Jane Miller, for example, said, "I wonder how I'll feel when my children are in school and our names are different. I suppose it will depend on where we live and how common it is for mothers to keep their own names (and how they've chosen to name their children)." Betty Franklin, who took back her birth name after her divorce, has a simple explanation for people who wonder why she and her children have different surnames. She just says that they have their father's name, and she has her father's name.

How the Children Feel

Women and men who are deciding what to name themselves and what to name their children should certainly be concerned about the effect on the children. This is particularly important if parents are considering giving their children a surname that is different from both parents'.

Most of the children of the participants in my study were affected only by their mothers' choice of name. Because most of the women had retained their birth names after marriage, regained them after divorce, or created new names, they had surnames different from their children's. Based upon the questionnaire responses, it seems that small children (preschool) accept this quite easily: They just recognize that "Mommy has a different name from Daddy and me."

Older children sometimes are bothered by the difference, since children tend to be very conformist and want to be just like everyone else. No one, however, mentioned this as being a big problem. One woman wrote, "My older son, when he noticed that my name wasn't like his friends' parents, wondered why, and thought we should be more conventional. But he's gotten used to it." Abigail K. Alcott said, "My sons were a little resentful at first — they thought I should use their surname. But they didn't put up much fuss, and I think they're secretly proud of my independent attitude."

When Carole Parker-Kramer hyphenated her name — using her birth name followed by her husband's name — both her daughters (ages 10 and 11) showed their support in a visible way: they decided to add her birth name as a middle name. One dropped her own middle name, and the other simply added a second middle name.

Occasionally children whose surnames differ from their mothers' have a problem in school. Mary B. Walker, who regained her birth name after being divorced, said, "The children didn't care at first until teachers at school began remarking how strange it was or concluding I was divorced twice." Janice Smith remembered experiences from her own childhood: "My parents were divorced when I was growing up and going through school. My mother remarried and had a different name, and I really felt disoriented when my teachers would ask who signed my report card. . . . If I had children, I would change my name to my husband's."

Some women who were divorced or widowed and then remarried kept their first husbands' surnames for the sake of their children. They felt that it would be comforting to the children to continue to share a name with their mothers. Linda Firestone-Bates, who hyphenated her first husband's name with her second husband's when she remarried, said, "My children were relieved, I think, to find I was retaining the name they were known by."

In situations where a woman has chosen a whole new surname, children's reactions vary. Eleanore Jay, who took her surname after divorce, said:

> My daughter was too young to understand at the time but I later explained to her why my name was different. She said "You can't do that." Once when I was renting a boat the man asked for my name. I gave it and my daughter, then age 7, said, "That's not her real name — she just made that up. You can't change your name unless you ask your mother!"

Two other women who took new surnames received a more positive reaction. "My kids were tolerant of the idea," wrote Andrea Papilion, "but thought I was a bit crazy (nothing new in that!)." Norma Goodwin Veridan's children were teenagers when she took a surname that combined her parents' names, and they approved of what she did: "My daughters were, and are, I believe, proud of me for doing something different and non-traditional that I believe in. My son said it was fine with him."

Probably the most potentially difficult situation for a child occurs when he is given a surname that is different from both parents'. Very few of the participants in my survey made this choice for their children's names, and I was not able to interview any of the children involved. However, I read an article in the February 11, 1987, *Wall Street Journal* about children's surnames in the 1980s. Teddy Roth-Tubman, then age 12, was one of the children interviewed. His parents, who both used their birth names, had given all three of their children different surnames, honoring various people who were meaningful to them. Teddy's surname honored writer Philip Roth and abolitionist Harriet Tubman.

Naming the Children

When asked if he liked having a name different from his parents, he said, "I guess so. It sure is a lot different than other kids." But he wouldn't do the same thing to his own children: "It's kind of peculiar," he said.

Conclusion

It is difficult to predict the future of children's surnames. There have been many suggestions in the past few years about "sex-neutral" schemes for naming children. The simplest solution is to hyphenate the parents' surnames — in alphabetical order, if there is a dispute. Or the parents can combine their surnames, if this is esthetically and linguistically possible. (Two ornate, polysyllabic names could produce an impossible jawbreaker for a child!) Another suggestion is that a child be given the surname of the parent of the same sex — a girl gets her mother's surname, a boy, his father's.

Sharon Lebell has formulated a new family naming system that she calls the Bilineal Solution. In this system, no one changes name at marriage; everyone keeps his or her name for life. A girl uses her mother's last name as a surname, and her father's last name as a middle name. A boy uses his father's last name as a surname, and his mother's last name as a middle name. By adopting this system, Lebell says, "nobody's name will ever again be the compulsory consequence of whom a woman or a mother happens to be married to at the time." It allows women's surnames, as well as men's, to be passed down the generations.[2]

Most of these solutions have been tried, with varying degrees of satisfaction, by people in my study. Each of them seems to have some flaws. Deciding which solution to implement remains a matter of personal choice. But whatever the choice, it needs to be implemented with common sense, and above all, with consideration for the children involved.

10. Problems in Business and Government

If you maintain or regain your birth name or if you take a new name, you may have problems with business, credit, or financial institutions, or with governmental agencies. Although it's not inevitable, it's possible. But cheer up. First of all, things now are much easier than they were 10 or 15 years ago. Second, there are ways to reduce, and sometimes to eliminate, these problems — you must be prepared, know your rights, and have the right attitude.

Financial Institutions

Institutions that handle money tend to look unfavorably upon anyone who uses a name different from the norm. "It won't fit in our computer," or "That's against our policy" are phrases that you may hear often from lower-level bank officials or credit card company employees. But unless you keep your savings under your mattress and always pay in cash, you have to deal with these institutions. Fortunately, few of them have a monopoly on the services that they provide, so you can shop around to find the ones that will be helpful, not obstructive.

Women who keep their own names have sometimes found it difficult to open joint checking or saving accounts with their husbands. A woman from suburban Boston said that when she was married in 1973, she and her husband had to go to five banks before they found one that would permit them to open a joint account in their own names. Another woman had to provide two notarized affidavits by friends and relatives stating that she had never used her husband's name for credit or employment. When faced with unnecessary trouble and delay in a situation like this, the best thing to do is to walk away. Simply make

93

some phone calls, find an institution that will meet your needs, and take your business there.

In the past ten years or so it appears that banks have become more flexible in accommodating couples with different surnames. When my husband and I lived in the Chicago area in the early 1980s, we had no problem in opening a joint checking account or in holding savings certificates jointly. I recently checked with officials at two large banks in Durham, North Carolina, where I now live, and they told me that they required no special procedures or documentation to open a joint account with two different names.

"But what do I do," you say, "if I have a checking account in my birth name and someone sends me a check in my husband's surname?" You can usually just deposit them. Once a month I receive a rent check payable to "Susan Adams" (I've been unable to train our renter that I'm not Adams), and I simply endorse it "Susan Adams (Susan J. Kupper)." My bank has never questioned this. One San Franciso woman, who uses her birth surname professionally and her husband's surname socially, was annoyed that bank tellers were constantly asking her if she wanted to change her name on her account. In a situation like this, where the inconvenience is momentary, don't waste your time being annoyed. Just say, "No thank you," and leave it at that.

Credit

Credit cards, the ubiquitous "plastic" that almost all of us carry, can often cause problems, too. In fact, the women in the survey had more difficulties with credit cards, charge accounts, and maintenance of credit records than with any other single area. Their specific problems related to names — getting the correct name on a credit card, getting a joint account with two different surnames, etc.

A good credit rating is an important issue for any woman, whatever name she uses. Before 1975, it was often a difficult credential to establish, especially for married women. Lenders tended to consider only a husband's income when making credit decisions, even if the wife's income was larger.

Frequently when a woman married and changed her name, she was asked to reapply for credit.[1] Thus, as Mary Smith, she may have paid her department store charge account on time for years. When she married and became Mary Johnson, the store apparently considered that the creditworthy Miss Smith no longer existed, and Mrs. Johnson had to submit another application for credit.

Women who were divorced or widowed frequently had a lot of trouble establishing or reestablishing their own credit history. Several women who were surveyed said that they had to start virtually from scratch in establishing credit after they were divorced and took back their birth names.

Congress tried to address some of these problems in 1975 with the Equal Credit Opportunity Act. Section 701 of the act states, "It shall be unlawful for any creditor to discriminate against any applicant, with respect to any aspect of a credit transaction . . . on the basis of . . . sex or marital status."[2] This law, along with the rules that the Federal Reserve Board has issued to creditors, assures a woman of some important credit rights. Among these is the right to designate the name in which a credit account is maintained. A woman may ask that an account be in her birth-given first and last names (Mary Smith), in her birth-given first name and husband's surname (Mary Johnson), or in a combined surname (Mary Smith Johnson). She is not required to indicate a "courtesy title" (Mrs., Ms., or Miss).

When a husband and wife open a joint account, the credit issuer is required to determine who will use the account and who is liable. If both husband and wife use the account, then the information on the account must be reported so that credit bureaus can set up separate accounts for the husband and wife. This assures a woman that she will have a credit record independent of her husband's.

The Equal Credit Opportunity Act and its associated rules also make it easier for a woman who has been divorced or widowed to keep her established sources of credit. Credit issuers cannot require her to reapply for credit on accounts that she and her husband held jointly — except when the credit was based only on her husband's income or credit rating and her own income at the time was not large enough to justify the credit.[3]

The women whom I surveyed mentioned a variety of problems that they had had relating to credit and names. Women who use hyphenated names sometimes received cards with their names amputated or mangled. When they complained, the credit card companies explained that their names were too long to fit or that the computer could not cope with a hyphen.

Married couples who wanted a credit account with one number, but cards with two different names, had to engage in a lot of explanation and correspondence to get it done right. Pat Schifler said, "Master-Card refused to give me a card of my own instead of using my husband's card until I argued them into the ground." Another woman said:

> The credit card company did not want to add me to my husband's card because I did not have the same last name. I threatened a discrimination lawsuit because if I had had the primary card and wanted to add him, they would not have insisted his name be the same as mine. They added me to my husband's card.

Sometimes the results of credit card applications were humorous, though annoying. Edith Lehman wrote, "I applied for a credit card in my name with my husband as an authorized user. The card was awarded, and sent to a fictitious individual — someone who had my husband's first name and my last name! It took a while to straighten it out." Even tangles like this represent progress. Several women found that ten or more years ago a credit card account with two names was difficult or sometimes impossible to obtain.

Some women, however, reported no problems in getting credit cards. "I've found credit cards to be surprisingly easy," wrote Ann Kelly. "Stores, oil companies, and MasterCard are all very willing to issue cards with separate names, both for joint accounts and for individual accounts which extend to spouses." Marilyn Burke, who went back to her birth surname after using her husband's surname for several years, said,

> I have had no problems, but I did put a certain amount of effort into changing my name on everything. With credit cards, I always filled out the forms for separate credit reports even on our joint accounts — this established a separate credit rating for me in my own name. (I would have done so even if I still used my husband's surname.) I have credit cards in my own name only, even though I haven't had a full-time job in five years. Companies sent these cards to me probably because of my separate credit rating and the fact that my husband and I own our own home.

In the nine years that I have been married, I have not had any difficulty in maintaining or obtaining credit. I had some credit cards before I was married, and never informed the companies that my marital status had changed, since my name remained the same. After

I got an American Express card and used it for several years, I requested an additional family member card for my husband. The company issued a card with his name on it, but billed to my account. (We did this because the annual fees are less than if we had two separate accounts.) When I asked for an additional gasoline company credit card for my husband, they issued it in my name. My husband signed his name on the back, and has used it ever since with no trouble. Probably my lack of problems is a good indication of how far women have come in the past ten years in gaining access to credit of their own — and in their own names.

Insurance and Mortgages

Insurance and mortgages are two other finance-related areas where some women mentioned having problems. Some found that their insurance companies were reluctant to include a spouse with a different name. Marybeth Grogan said that her husband was almost denied inclusion on her auto insurance policy until "I raised a bit of ruckus." Joan Alexander wrote, "Blue Cross-Blue Shield practically insisted that I use my husband's name on the policy. I refused — it was my policy originally." I was particularly interested in Joan's comment, because my husband and I recently got health insurance from Blue Cross-Blue Shield, though in a different state than she did. The policy is in my husband's name, and we had no problem in listing me as a dependent, using my birth name. My husband simply had to sign a form certifying that I am a qualified participant in his policy.

As Marybeth and Joan found, sometimes it's necessary to be very firm with insurance companies. It may be more convenient for them if everyone on a policy has the same name, but if you and your husband have different surnames, then the companies must cope. It appears from some of the responses in the survey that some insurance agents are still afraid that there will be legal problems if a couple uses different surnames on an insurance policy. Assure them that this is not so, and insist that your names be listed correctly. Otherwise, you are sure to have problems when you submit claims.

You also must be firm when dealing with mortgage companies. Some women found that when they applied for mortgages with their husbands, they had to be very insistent about having the mortgages issued in their separate names, rather than in the names of Mr. and Mrs. Husband. I suspect that this is less of a problem today than it was ten or more years ago. When my husband and I obtained mortages in 1982 and again in 1985, neither lender questioned issuing the mortgage in the names of Richard D. Adams and Susan J. Kupper.

Government — Some General Comments

There is one disadvantage to dealing with government: you can't take your business elsewhere if you're dissatisfied. There's only one driver's license bureau (for your state), one Social Security Administration, and one Internal Revenue Service, and each agency operates under certain regulations and laws. Many of the women in my survey did have some difficulties with government agencies when they retained, regained, or changed their names. There are, however, things that you can do to minimize these problems. Here are a few guidelines, based upon the experiences of the women in the survey, my own experiences, and conversations with government officials.

First, be prepared — find out beforehand what paperwork and identification you will need to bring or send to the agency. You'll save yourself time and aggravation this way.

Second, be reasonable. It's irritating when a government official insists upon a lot of paperwork, and sometimes all the forms may be unnecessary. But if you've changed your name, for whatever reason, the government needs to make sure that no fraud is involved, and this is generally why they may ask for legal documentation of the change.

Third, be consistent in the name you use. In general, don't use your birth surname in one place and your husband's surname in another. Some women divide their name use into "personal" and "professional" spheres. If you want to do this and are willing to cope with the occasional confusion that may result, that's fine. But make sure that you always use the same name in all dealings with government. It is particularly important to use a consistent name where you work (the name that goes on your paychecks), with Social Security, and with the Internal Revenue Service.

Federal Government

Some of the women whom I surveyed had name-related problems in dealing with agencies of the federal government: the Social Security Administration, Internal Revenue Service, Passport Office, and Postal Service.

"Social Security threatened that I'd never receive my benefits without a legal change of name, which is why I filed it in court," wrote Anne Bernique. (She started using her birth name again after her divorce.) Elaine Masters, who took back her birth name in her divorce decree, noted that "Social Security was the only agency which insisted upon seeing the legal decree."

Today they no longer require you to show a court-prepared document to get a Social Security card in a new name. You must fill out an Application for Change form (available from any Social Security office) and show identification in your old and new names. If you've changed your name by statute or divorce decree, bring along the legal document. If you've changed your name by common law (without going through the court system), it's helpful to bring a notarized statement to this effect. Most important, make sure that you inform Social Security of any name change.

The name (and its associated number) that you have on file with Social Security is very important. Not only is it the name under which you accumulate Social Security benefits, it is the name by which the Internal Revenue Service identifies you. If the IRS records list you as Mary S. Johnson (your married name) and you file your income tax return as Mary Smith (your birth name), you'll have a problem.

Karen Laplante discovered this for herself. "Our federal income tax return 'bounced' because the names on the form did not agree with Social Security records," she wrote. S. JoAnne Clarke had a similar experience:

> My husband's accountant made out our joint return to James R. and S. JoAnne Clarke Andrews. When I had to sign it, I protested to my husband that I never had used that name; he was irritated and thought I was making an unnecessary scene—so I signed it. Sure enough, two months later I received an official letter from the IRS, wondering whether I was falsely using a name not on my Social Security records! I wrote back and explained about my husband's accountant—apparently that passed muster, as I heard no more from them. The next year I just signed S. JoAnne Clarke.

My husband and I had a similar problem with our accountant, who listed our names on our joint return as Richard D. and Susan K. Adams. When Richard told him that wasn't my name, our accountant said the IRS expected married women to have the same last names as their husbands. Richard then told him that both he and the IRS needed to change their expectations and got him to correct it.

Other women had name-related problems with the IRS, too:

> It took the IRS about three years to get the name label correct on the joint form my husband and I used.

> I continue to get notices from the federal government that I have not filed taxes for earlier years based on confusion about last name.

> Our joint tax return was sent back to us — we were told that I must file using the name Maureen Kerr Whitley. My husband and I both talked to many IRS representatives and finally resolved the problem. I will file using Maureen Kerr.

> The IRS and state government issued tax refunds to my spouse and me, using the same surname — HIS. We returned the checks for three years for reissuance in our correcct names before the matter was resolved.

I don't know the details of these situations, and so I can't tell whether the problems could have been resolved more quickly. Sometimes when dealing with the IRS, trying to get a record changed or corrected can be like swimming through molasses. But persevere. As long as the government is going to take your tax money, the least they can do is take it from you under the correct name.

A few women whom I surveyed complained of problems in getting or renewing their passports. Denise Anderson, who took back her birth name after divorce, said that when she renewed her passport, "I should have kept my mouth shut and there would have been no trouble. I should have said 'single' instead of 'divorced.' They wanted both my marriage license and divorce papers to show my two name changes!" Linda Canoli-Lerner said, "The Passport Office insisted on a copy of my dissolution decree allowing me to drop my second husband's name."

As Denise and Linda found, the Department of State (which issues passports) is particular that a passport applicant be able to prove her identity. A United States passport entitles the bearer to certain rights and protections all over the world, and the State Department doesn't want a person using one fraudulently. The good news is that getting the name you want on your passport is much easier than it used to be. If you are married, use your birth name, and have identification (driver's license, etc.) in this name, you will have no trouble in getting a passport issued in this name.

Changing the name on your passport is not very difficult, either. Assume, for example, that Mary Smith is divorced and took back her birth name through her divorce decree or a statutory name change. She wants to renew her passport, which was issued in her married name, Mary Johnson. In order to get a new passport as Mary Smith, she must bring three documents: 1) a certified copy of her divorce decree or legal name change; 2) an amendment form (available at passport offices or main post offices); and 3) her present passport.

If Mary Smith took back her birth name by common law, she should bring in the amendment form and her present passport. She can then be issued a new passport as "Mary Smith, a/k/a (also known as) Mary Johnson." (Sometimes local passport officials don't know about this, and they may have to check with the passport office in Washington, D.C.) A woman who hyphenates her surname with her husband's can get a new passport in her hyphenated surname without an a/k/a.

After Eleanor Jay was divorced, she adopted a new surname by common law. Now, she said, "I cannot get a passport because they require a legal change of name and I strongly object to having to go through the courts to get permission to exercise my rights. I have been unable to think of a way to circumvent this requirement."

I don't know how long ago Eleanor tried to get a passport. If she tried again today, she would probably have no trouble, unless she objected to being "a/k/a."

I would not have thought that the U.S. Postal Service would care what name a woman used, as long as her mail had stamps and zip codes on it. But a few women did encounter opposition from postal personnel. "The post office really fought my use of my name," wrote Marilyn Taylor. "They insisted that two names are not allowed on a mailbox." This was in a small town in Georgia. In another small town, this time in Alaska, Sharon Reutman said:

> The postmistress gets upset with my husband and me because she has to look in two different spots when a package comes in, either under

101

'R' or 'D.' I never thought this was a problem when we were living together, but after we married she made several comments. I believe it was her way of saying she doesn't understand why I kept my name.

Picking up mail from the post office was occasionally annoying, too. "The post office wouldn't give me any mail mistakenly addressed to me with my husband's surname because I had no ID which read that way," one woman said. Another said, "The post office frequently refuses to turn over packages to me that are addressed to my husband. I've taken to carrying a signed authorization with me."

My husband had an interesting experience picking up our mail after returning from a vacation. A clerk did not want to give him mail addressed to Susan Kupper. Questioning that we were married, he asked, "If you're married, why don't you and she have the same last name?" My husband simply replied, "We had different fathers." He came home with all the mail.

State and Local Government

The most serious problems that my survey participants had with state and local governments involved voter registration and drivers' licenses. Some of the experiences they described were 10 or 15 years ago, though, and many states have changed their laws and policies since then.

In 1879 Lucy Stone was refused the right to vote in her own name, and American women have had an uphill battle ever since to assert this right. Starting in the 1920s, many states instituted laws requiring that upon marriage a woman had to re-register to vote under her husband's surname. Judith Greenberg, who lives in Ohio, discovered this: "When we got married in 1976, my voter registration was automatically changed, and it was a pain changing it back." A Tennessee resident, Elizabeth Hales, sidestepped a similar law. She said, "In my state, *by law*, a woman is required to register to vote in her married name. I avoided this simply by registering before marriage."

These were the only two comments about voter registration by women in my study, and this issue is evidently less of a problem than it used to be. One factor is very likely the decision in the 1972 Maryland case, *Stuart v. Board of Supervisors of Elections*. The Maryland Court of Appeals ruled that Mary Stuart, who kept her birth name after marriage, had the right to register to vote in this name. (See Chapter 1.) This influential case and others that followed probably caused many states to alter their voter registration procedures.

There have also been considerable changes in state policies about drivers' licenses. In the past, though, many women have found it difficult, if not impossible, to get a driver's license in their birth or other chosen names instead of their husbands' names. Muriel Marlowe, who married in the late 1960s, said that Maryland would only recognize her husband's surname as legal, so that is the name that appears on her driver's license, even though she never uses it otherwise.

A 1972 Supreme Court decision (*Forbush v. Wallace*) gave support to states that required a married woman to use her husband's name on her driver's license unless she changed her name by statutory procedures. When Wendy Forbush challenged such an Alabama law, both a lower court and the U.S. Supreme Court ruled against her. (See Chapter 1.)

In the mid-1970s other women in my study had trouble getting drivers' licenses in the names they wished. Rebecca Parker Elgin, for example, added her birth surname to her ex-husband's name after she got divorced. But, she said, "the Michigan Driver's License Bureau did not let me change it."

In some cases, persistence helped women to get the name they wanted on their drivers' licenses. Anne Falken-Carrerra said, "The state of New Mexico (or at least the person I was dealing with) was very adamant that I could not keep my maiden name on the driver's license, and even refused to hyphenate it, but I finally won." Edith Bliss-Delaney wrote, "The Louisiana Driver's License Bureau workers insisted for two days that Bliss-Delaney wasn't a legal last name, even though I'd had it for two years then. A call to the state office made them grudgingly accept it."

A little creativity worked sometimes, too. Eleanor Jay, who changed the name on her Delaware driver's license, wrote:

> They didn't want to do it at all, especially when they found out that I had made the name up. However, I bullied the clerk into giving me a form they had which had to be notarized (my one concession to the law) which was meant for divorced women to return to their original name. I crossed off "maiden" and put "chosen."

103

In the years since the Forbush case, many states have responded to court challenges or other pressures by changing their laws or agency regulations. In fact, in 1982 the Alabama Supreme Court repudiated the Forbush case in *State v. Taylor*. The latter was a case concerning a woman's right to vote in her own name.

North Carolina provides a good example of this gradual change. In 1972, Patricia Kapp, who took part in my survey, discovered a law similar to the one challenged by Wendy Forbush in Alabama. "The state of North Carolina refused to give me a driver's license in my birth name," she wrote. "I had to get it in my husband's name unless I had a court order allowing me to change my name legally to my own." About five years later the situation had improved somewhat. When Jane Greiman applied for a driver's license, she said, "I was required to sign an affidavit stating that my legal surname was not that of my husband in North Carolina. This required an additional 30 minutes for a five-minute process." By 1984, a married woman didn't have to do anything special to have her birth name on her North Carolina driver's license.

Today different states vary somewhat in their requirements about drivers' licenses. If you are married and use your birth name, you should have no trouble obtaining or renewing a driver's license in this name. If you are taking back your birth name or changing your name other than by marriage, you can show a divorce decree, legal name change, or notarized affidavit stating that you have changed your name. (You can use the last if you have changed your name by common law. It will be effective in most states, though probably not in all. See Chapter 12.)

If you want to register to vote, get a driver's license, or have some other dealing with your state or local government that involves name change, it is best to know your rights and know the law first. You can go to a local law library and look up the relevant state laws. Or call your local bar association or the nearest office of the American Civil Liberties Union. Then you will be armed with the facts if you encounter any opposition from officials.

When you know your rights, you will be able to handle problems politely but firmly. This seems to work well for Andrea Borland:

> Bureaucrats and clerical people often try to insist on listing me under
> my husband's name. Speaking to them gently but firmly usually settles

the problem. Businesses which persist in addressing me as "Mrs. Husband" get two letters of explanation and a third telling them why they have just lost our patronage. Government employees have always responded to either explanations or a stony refusal to yield the point. So far, I've had no major hassles.

Attitude

I think it is important not to anticipate problems. There is a good chance that you won't encounter any. In fact, about a third of the women in the survey reported that they had had no problems in using their chosen names. In this area, as in so many others, attitude is crucial. The women who had the fewest difficulties were generally the ones who took a matter-of-fact attitude. Elaine Grover-Martin, for example, wrote:

> Commercial institutions accept my hyphenated name because I'm credit-worthy. Government agencies accept my hyphenated name because I am a lawyer of some visibility in the community and I presume they respect my decision. (They probably think I wouldn't use a name unless it were legal.)

There is also no need to make speeches about your name. Some women who used their birth names mentioned that many businesses with which they dealt were not even aware that they were married. Jessica Baker said, "In some cases, I might have trouble if I told them Baker was my maiden name and different from my husband's — so I don't volunteer that information. If they ask my husband's name, I tell them; if not, I just give my own name."

Barbara Kmiec offers some admirably simple and common-sense advice about women and their names:

> I think women have problems when they assume a defensive posture. If a woman says "this is my name" without any actions to make anyone think she is doing something out of the ordinary, they will accept her name as naturally as she does. If she broadcasts in any way that what she is doing is not the usual way, others will pick up on it and want to know why. The key to *hassle-free* use of the name of her choice is not "to assert publicly her right to use her own name," but simply to use it without fanfare.

105

11. Other Problems

> When we rented a house, the owner wanted to be sure we were married and requested to see our license. Since we had different names, he was suspicious.

> The biggest problem was with the obstetrician's office, where they insisted that I *must* use my husband's name to eliminate confusion in the hospital when the baby was born.

> The chairman of my company continually explains my name and that it is different from my husband's. This is *very* awkward in a business situation.

The participants in my study reported a variety of name-related problems in areas other than business or government. Whether they didn't change their names at marriage, took back their birth names, or changed to new names, some women ran into opposition from their employers, co-workers, landlords, doctors, lawyers, or others. Fortunately, these were generally aggravating, rather than traumatic, experiences.

About 10 percent of the women in the study reported that their employers disapproved of their name choices. Some resisted when women did not change to their husbands' surnames after marriage:

> My employer at that time was traditional. He didn't like it and insisted on using my husband's name.

> Initially my boss insisted on introducing me by my husband's name — it took several requests and reminders (over a period of a year!) before he caught on and respected my desire to use my name.

> One employer asked "why?" and what did my husband think of this!

> After getting married I arrived at work to find a new nameplate on my desk. I had told my boss I wanted to keep my birth name but I was told to keep the nameplate "in case I change my mind."

When Rose Catherine Callahan *did* change her name (she went back to her birth name after divorce), her employer didn't like it. She wrote, "My employer bellyached about new cards, door labels, directory, financial records, etc., but he finally complied."

Judith Weichinger is a minister who kept her birth name after marriage. She said:

> As a pastor, I see how conservative the church is. In interviews, I would not mention my husband, John Randall, but my husband John. I wanted them to know me and my gifts before automatically saying they weren't interested. Only when I knew a church was interested in me would I bring up the issue. I know there are people in the congregation who feel uncomfortable with my "role model," but I'm convinced once they get to know me, *maybe* they'll see it differently.

Faye Thayer, who works for the federal goverment, was the only woman whose name decision actually pleased her employer: "My administrative officer was happy when she found out I was *not* changing my name when I got married. She didn't have to file all the name-changing forms for the government."

Some women met with disapproval — and cliches — from their co-workers when they kept their birth names or hyphenated their names. "My co-workers tend to label me a 'women's libber,'" wrote Eleanor Herman, "and they view all my actions through that label." Judy Frank-Coppelson, a school social worker, reported, "Two male teachers mumbled something about 'feminist' and asked what my husband thought. I told them, but I don't think they understood." Patricia Kolben-Andreoli used her husband's surname for two years and then hyphenated her name. She wrote: "After I continuously used the hyphenated name for four years, 80 percent of the employees continue to say 'Mrs. Andreoli.' Surprisingly, older women are the worst. I get comments like 'Which name do you want to use?' or 'You should be proud of your husband's name.' or 'Oh, she's a women's libber.'"

Judith Weichinger said: "The man I minister with does not like the fact that I retained my name. (He hates Ms. and is glad he can call me Reverend.) But he respects my opinion and as far as I know does not denigrate me behind my back."

Sheri Heller-Wayne's co-workers came up with a different reason she should take her husband's name: "Some co-workers expressed the opinion that since I had not 'made a name' for myself under my maiden name, there was no need to keep it."

A few women who took part in my study reported that their names caused a problem — or at least a question — to arise with their landlords. Emily Stanton, who kept her birth name, wrote, "A woman who managed a house we rented while living in Illinois demanded to see our marriage certificate and even then refused to put the house in both our names since I would not sign with my husband's surname. She would only put my husband's name on the lease." Kass Sheedy said, "When my husband and I married we wanted our apartment lease to be in both names. The landlord required that I get an affidavit stating that this was legal." Other women described similar situations, and one took it rather lightly: "Our landlords are very traditional and were concerned about our actually being married, since they did not want anyone moving in who might set a bad example for their daughters by 'living in sin!' We swore we were married and there has been no problem, but we found this amusing."

Hospitals and doctors seem to be quite inflexible when dealing with two-name families. Ann Pickett usually uses her birth name. However, she wrote, "The HMO in which I am enrolled is through my husband's employment, and they couldn't seem to process my membership as long as I had a different name. So for that particular bureaucracy I'm Mrs. Paulson." Jeanette Glass did the same thing: "My medical coverage is a family plan under my husband's name. I found it too complicated to keep medical records in my name, so with the clinic I use my husband's name."

Some women don't even try to straighten things out. "Hospitals and Blue Cross are generally confused," wrote one. "I have medical records and bills in all possible combinations of names."

Women had particular difficulty with hospitals when they had babies. Sharon Sterling said, "I had to show our marriage license at the hospital where our baby was born, so the baby could have my husband's last name." (This occurred in a Chicago hospital in 1981.) Other women wrote:

> I did have some problems when my baby was born, convincing the hospital that my husband and I were married and that the child would be taking my husband's name.

109

> I had no problems except with the hospital when my baby was born. The lady in records complained about how much work I was making for her!

Jane Clements had a good solution for dealing with a recalcitrant health professional. She wrote, "I had a problem with my dentist, who insisted on transferring my records to my 'real' name. I transferred myself to a more cooperative dentist!"

Lawyers and judges caused a problem for a few women. In most instances it was not that the lawyer or judge did not know the law; it was that he wanted to impose his opinions and biases upon the woman involved. In Melissa Townsend's case, when she got divorced, she wanted to take an old family name as her surname. The divorce judge, she said, called her name change "an adolescent search for identity, evidence of hatred of my ex-husband and my own father, an indication of instability and 'bizarre' behavior, and an effort to cut my children's father out of their lives." The judge who granted Susan Selleck a divorce was equally blunt — and prejudiced: "He indicated my marriage would have worked had I changed my name, even though I had previously testified I left for other reasons."

When Marni Politte Harmony and her husband, Peter, chose their surname (Harmony), the judge who heard their request for name change didn't care for it. "The judge was critical of our decision and grilled us like naughty children who were thoughtless regarding their families' feelings."

Some lawyers and judges worried that if women took back their birth names, their children would be adversely affected:

> I wanted to go back to my birth name after I got divorced. But my lawyer talked me out of it because of the children — whatever that meant.

> The judge at the divorce when my name was changed was concerned that my name would differ from the child of that marriage. I never did understand why it would make any difference. He did, however, go ahead and grant the change.

As recently as July 1988, a United States district court judge in Pittsburgh demonstrated overt bias against an attorney in his courtroom who used her birth name. Judge Hubert Teitelbaum told Barbara

Wolvovitz, "From here on, in this courtroom you will use Mrs. Lobel. That's your name." (Wolvovitz is married to University of Pittsburgh law professor Jules Lobel.) When she refused, he threatened her with jail. After the judge's comments received a lot of publicity, he finally apologized. "I recognize your right to be addressed in any manner in which you see fit," he told Wolvovitz, "and I apologize for my comments." He also said he was mistaken in telling her that state law required her to use her husband's surname unless she had approval from the court.[1]

A few women had minor problems when traveling with their husbands. Gail Galvin said that "some travel agents seem reluctant to book rooms under two names." Others wrote:

> We had slight trouble when applying for visas to Central American countries and when purchasing plane tickets under married status, but with different surnames. This seemed to have more to do with verifying identity than with any disapproving attitude, however.

> When returning from an overseas trip, the customs inspector would not allow us to pool our husband/wife exemption until we showed copies of our marriage license and my change-of-name court order.

Judith Weichinger and her husband had no difficulties, however: "We did expect problems traveling in England and Scotland, staying in small bed and breakfasts. We had inquiries and people thought we were weird, but no one kicked us out. (We even took our marriage license, but never had to show it.)"

Some women reported name-related problems in other areas. Kit Carlson, for example, wrote: "The occasions when I have felt most threatened by others about my choice of name usually come when dealing with religious organizations or people. I really believe in my marriage and I have a strong faith (not fundamentalist, though). But the priest who married us, the people at a Marriage Encounter we took, and other religious types always hassle us."

Doris Paschen had trouble enrolling in graduate school: "West Texas State University's registrar refused to admit me unless I used my husband's name. So I called the university's president, who happened to be a friend, and he got it all fixed in about 15 minutes!"

Cathy Stone Wilson uses both surnames without a hyphen. When she first started using this name, she said, "I had a lot of trouble. It is somewhat easier now that all my identification has my new name. People (especially women) would say awful things like 'Is that your name?' or 'Yes, but I need your real name,' or 'Is it necessary to have both last names?' I think most of the problem was space — my name didn't fit in the blank."

Many women mentioned the social awkwardness or confusion that can result when a husband and wife have different names. People may not realize that the couple are married, they may call the husband by his wife's surname (or vice versa), or the couple may be given matching — and therefore incorrect — name tags.

> Name tags are a drag. I often have to rewrite name tags at community events, especially if I am with my husband.

> It is often awkward socially for people who meet my husband first; they have trouble remembering my name and are embarrassed. Names become a point you must make.

> I sometimes feel self-conscious and feel a need to clarify that my husband and I are really married.

> Psychological disadvantage: the recurring hurt when a close relative or friend introduces me as 'Mrs. _____' or when another relative 'can't remember' my husband's name.

When there are two names in a family, there also can be other minor irritations in dealing with stores, doctors' offices, and other businesses:

> It occasionally creates confusion — explaining to the pediatrician's nurse that my name is not the same as my son's, and trying to remember whose name the dog is under at the vet's.

> When my husband takes our car in for repairs, he uses his name — Allen. When I pick it up, I have to say, 'Is my car ready? The name is Allen,' even though I sign the check with my own surname, Connolly.

Finally, one woman noted what may be the worst aspect of all to a two-name household: getting double portions of junk mail!

Luck, Geography, and Attitude

As you read this litany of problems — some serious and some trivial — don't be discouraged. Remember that a third of the women in my study said that they had had *no* problems with their names. It appears to me that problems, or lack of them, depend upon three main factors: luck, geographical location, and attitude.

If you're lucky, you won't run into a cranky, suspicious landlord, a highly traditional employer, or a misogynistic judge. In many instances, whether you have problems just depends upon the individuals with whom you have to interact.

Where you live also makes a difference. Many of the women I studied live in or near some of the largest metropolitan areas in the United States — New York, Boston, Washington, Chicago, San Francisco, and Los Angeles. Because of their size and diversity, these metropolitan areas are more anonymous and tolerant of deviations from the social norms than are smaller towns or rural areas. One woman, who lives in Boston and grew up in New York, commented, "Boston is not exactly 'middle America' in terms of social mores; neither is New York." A Boston-area physician said, "Using one's own name is such a common occurrence in medicine that I don't think 'nontraditional' is accurate, at least in this part of the country."

Several women mentioned the difficulties of moving from one of these large cities to one that is smaller and less cosmopolitan. An attorney in her early thirties said:

> I lived for two years with my daughter and husband in Washington D.C., where many professional women seem to keep their names, so that two-name families are common (and not for reasons of divorce and such). There the social situation wasn't too difficult. Now we live in Wilmington, Delaware, where I'm the exception, not the rule. More people seem confused and I'm more defensive and uncertain.

Lauren Pisano, who moved from California to Delaware in the mid-1970s, made somewhat similar comments:

> My husband and I met in California. I am a California native; he is an Easterner. We lived together for five years in a community of mostly previously divorced people living with others. There and then, it was the norm for a woman to use her own name. At this point, we migrated

East to a very traditional community. No woman I met had her own name. I was considered weird anyway (clothes, lifestyle, politics, etc.), so people we met either assumed we weren't married or that I was a women's libber.

In the South, even in urban areas, it appears to be less accepted and less common for women to keep their own names than in the large cities of the Northeast, Midwest, or West Coast. Beverly Camp, who lives in New Orleans, wrote:

The situations in which I have encountered the greatest resistance have been social ones. The absolute worst is in our current neighborhood, a "nice" WASP upper middle-class haven from crime. In our nice, safe neighborhood, tolerance of social differences isn't high on the scale of priorities. So they wouldn't print our names as "we would like to welcome Bob Kramer and Beverly Camp" for fear someone would think (God forbid) that we were POSSLQ (Persons of the Opposite Sex Sharing Living Quarters)! Oh, NO! So they said "we'd like to welcome Bob Kramer and his wife Beverly..." All I can say is, at least I got my first name in and wasn't buried under "Mr. and Mrs. Bob Kramer."

Rachel Crandall and her husband, David Robinson, both in their forties, created a stir when they bought a house in Columbia, South Carolina:

My husband and I apparently caused a minor uproar when we moved into a rather conservative neighborhood. The previous owner had apologized to the neighbors for selling a house to a woman who was apparently living with a man. She further explained that Crandall and Robinson were not "bad" names, and she thought we might get married or at least be fairly orderly because she thought with such "good" names, we must not be "white trash." The neighbors seemed to be curious, but not worried; they were just glad we weren't black.

Some Southerners have had very few problems. One woman who took back her birth name during her marriage stated that she found the whole process surprisingly easy, "even in provincial and traditional Nashville." Another said, "When I lived in Dallas I was praised for my actions, except among church people. But when I moved to the country I met open hostility."

Women in rural areas who use their birth names or hyphenated names have the most difficulty in gaining acceptance for their choices, as these areas tend to be more conservative and homogeneous than large cities. In a community where most people know each other, they tend to look askance at anything unconventional, or at least talk about it a lot. Ann Le Compte, who lives in South Dakota, said: "Neighbors in this small, rural community questioned whether we were legally married, but the gossip up the road cleared up that controversy after she actually *saw* our wedding photos."

Janice Hamilton, living in a semi-rural area in Georgia, said:

> In this small town (where people know both me and my husband), they do give me some grief. However, at least more people seem to know "someone else like you" now and the only real problem is a *big* concern about whether to call me "Miss" or "Mrs." (I don't care.) In the South, Ms. ("Mizz") is 100 years old, anyway.

Wherever you live, your attitude can make a big difference in whether you have problems with your name. Yes, you have a right to use whatever name you wish, and you should insist on that if necessary. Cathy Stone Wilson said, "I don't have as many problems now and I think it is in large part due to assertiveness on my part. I get real adamant about my name." But don't be defensive or make a big issue about things that are not important. Susan Ransom, for example, is irritated because "some utilities, the phone company, and other organizations refuse to put both our names on our accounts. They claim the computer can handle only one, and always choose my husband's name. I objected, and argued that with one command they can change the computer specifications. No effect at all."

Is this important enough to make a fuss about? Put some of the utilities in your name, and some in your husband's. Then you'll each have evidence for your separate credit histories, if that's your concern.

In an ideal world, names and changing them would never cause a problem. But in this less-than-ideal world, you'll have to cope with an occasional problem. Consider making it as simple for yourself as possible. Try to be consistent with the name you use, so you don't end up with bureaucratic tangles in insurance or taxes. Let the occasional needling comment pass without becoming outraged. If you're going to be in a situation where you think your name might be questioned, carry a copy of your marriage license, as Nancy Lawton does. She said that the single problem she's had is "sometimes my husband and I are not recognized as legitimate partners when, for example, I need to sign for him or represent him in some way. In most cases, I feel this is very legitimate; businesses, etc. need to protect themselves. I simply carry a copy of our marriage certificate."

Finally, recognize that you may meet with an unexpected problem. Joan McGarrigle, a sports fan in Denver who took back her birth name, encountered one. "Believe it or not," she wrote, "the most paperwork involved in changing my name with credit cards, property, employer, driver's license, etc., was in changing my name on my Denver Broncos season ticket!"

12. Women's Names — The Law

If you're about to get married, or divorced, or are just not happy with the name you bear now, you have the opportunity to use the name you want. And it's legal. In fact, the right to choose a name originates in English common law, which is followed in all states except Louisiana. (Common law is the legal system that originated in England, and is in effect in most countries colonized by England. It is based upon court decisions, customs, and usages, rather than upon codified written laws. Louisiana, having been colonized by France, is governed by civil law.)

The common law says that you may use any surname that you wish, as long as you have no fraudulent purpose. (This means you can't use a name to conceal your identity to avoid debts, for example.) You may also change your name at any time without going to court. The name change laws in each state exist only to help you exercise this common law right. They provide a way to make an official record of your change of name.

Keeping Your Birth Name

If you have the common law right to change your name, then you have the right *not* to change it. Attorney Priscilla Ruth MacDougall, who is the country's leading expert on women's and children's legal name rights, states clearly: "Consistent with the right to change one's name is the right not to change it at marriage as most women traditionally have done."[1]

Although this right has always existed, it has not always been recognized by the American court system. Until quite recently, many women have encountered legal problems when they kept their birth names after marriage. Two examples that I've discussed in earlier chapters are the cases of *Forbush v. Wallace* (in which an Alabama

117

woman was not allowed to have a driver's license in her birth name) and *Stuart v. Board of Supervisors of Elections* (in which a woman had to take her case to the Maryland Supreme Court to be able to register to vote in her birth name). Two other cases, each of which set an important precedent, further illustrate the difficulties that women had in the early to mid-1970s.

In 1972, Priscilla MacDougall brought suit in Madison, Wisconsin, to establish her right to use her birth name. (She was married, but had not changed her name.) At the time, she was an assistant attorney general, and her impetus for bringing this test case came when she heard about the *Forbush v. Wallace* decision. Though MacDougall went through a great deal of harassment in the process, she did finally win her own case.

Another Wisconsin case was important in establishing women's name rights. Kathleen Rose Harney was a teacher in Milwaukee who did not change her name when she married. In 1973 the school board there told her that she would have to take her husband's surname (Kruzel) or get a court-ordered name change to Harney. When Harney took this to court, Judge Ralph Podell of the Milwaukee Circuit Court agreed with the school board. He stated that there was no written statute on this question, but that the custom of women taking their husbands' surnames had "ripened into a rule of common law." Podell wrote further, "This court has great concern for the stability of the family and feels very strongly that family unity also requires that all members bear the same legal name." He worried about the effect of Harney's action on her future children, and said it would be better for the couple to decide on one name or not get married at all.[2]

Harney appealed the case, and in 1975 the Wisconsin Supreme Court ruled in her favor. It stated that women need not change their names when they marry and married couples need not have the same surname. Further, the court said, common law had never required a woman to take her husband's surname.[3]

Many states used to have laws that made it difficult or impossible for women to keep their birth names after marriage without getting a court-ordered "name change." Today, however, the situation is different. In an article published in 1985, Priscilla MacDougall wrote, "By statute, judicial opinion, state attorney general opinion, formal and informal agency directives or memoranda, or legislation, all states now recognize that women have the right to not change their names when they marry."[4]

So if you don't want to change your name when you get married, don't do it. Keep your driver's license, Social Security card, credit cards, etc., just as they are. File your taxes jointly with your husband (if you choose to), take out a mortgage or get insurance together — just do it in both names: Joe Smith and Nancy Jones. You're not likely to have any legal problems today. As I've indicated in several chapters, I found it very easy not to change my name when I married in 1980. In fact, I didn't have to do anything at all.

You can even use two names — your birth name in business and professional activities and your husband's surname socially or in private life. However, the question arises, where do you draw the line between the two? Is a driver's license part of your social or business life? Should you have one credit card in your birth name for business expenses and one in your husband's surname for personal expenses? And so on. There is no question that you *do* have the common law right to use two names. However, in some states you may encounter resistance from the state government if you want to use more than one name in their various records.

Regaining Your Birth Name or Changing to a New Name

If you want to take back your birth name or use a new name, there are three possible methods: you can have the change indicated in your divorce decree, make a statutory name change, or change your name by common law.

Many women who decide to take back their birth names after divorce have the change listed in their divorce decrees. This gives them an easy way of providing "legal proof" of their name when they have to get new identification. Some do this while at the same time grumbling that it shouldn't be necessary (it's not). As jan gardner [sic] wrote, "I changed my name informally by ceasing to use any other name 10 years ago. When I divorced two years ago my lawyer insisted on including a name change in the decree 'to make it legal.' No legal process was required to change it when I married. I think we should be able to change our names back as easily as when we marry!"

A second choice to regain your birth name or take a new name is to follow the procedures for a statutory name change. Every state has a law governing change of name, and usually the procedures are not terribly difficult. If you want to check the law in your state, you could go to a local law library, perhaps at a university. Local women's groups may be able to help you. The American Civil Liberties Union chapter in your area will most likely have name change information, too.

To find an example, I looked up the name change law in North Carolina, where I live, and found that it is similar to those in some other states.[5] A woman (this applies to men also) who wishes to change her name has to file an application with the clerk of the superior court in her county, after first publishing notice of this intention for 10 days. In the application she must state her "true name," where and when she was born, her parents' names, the name she wants to adopt and her reasons for this, and whether she's ever changed her name "by law" before. She must also file affidavits from two people attesting to her good character.

If the clerk of court then decides that "good and sufficient reason exists for the change of name," he orders the change to be made and recorded. The applicant can then get certified copies of the order to use in changing her Social Security records, drivers' license, and other records. Helen Langer, who took back her birth name by statute in California, found this kind of document to be very useful. She wrote, "At the time of name change I advise getting a dozen or more notarized (or "court-verified") copies of the legal order. These have saved me many hassles in dealing with government agencies in this and other countries."

North Carolina's law does not guarantee that a person's application for name change will be granted; the decision is left to the discretion of the court. A 1975 North Carolina decision denying a woman's request to regain her birth name stated, "The court is not subject to the whim or capricious desire of a petitioner to change his name."[6] But what can you do if a judge does refuse your application? Priscilla Mac-Dougall thinks that any name change request that is denied will probably be reversed on appeal.

Obtaining a statutory name change is not generally a difficult process, and unless your request is highly unusual, you're not likely to run into many snags today. Ten or more years ago, however, that was not always the case. Lania Groleau, who changed to a completely new name in the mid-1970s, told me about her experiences:

> While filling out all the forms, an older male bureaucrat told me I had to get my husband's signature on the form before he would file it. There

was no space on the form for this, but he insisted, and wouldn't give me a reason. Fuming, I went back home, got Peter's signature, took more time off from work, and brought the forms back to the office. I brought all the papers to another office worker — a woman this time — and asked her why I had to get my husband's signature. She said, "Oh, you don't need it — some of the men around here like to give you a hard time." (Not a direct quote, but this is the gist of what she said.)

At the court hearing itself [for name change], the judge — a man — told me that I would mess up my child psychologically by changing my name because it would be different from his. "You don't know how many women come in here years later to change their child's name, too." This didn't make any sense to me, but I didn't say anything because this man had the power to deny me my own name. I kept quiet and he changed my name legally. But still today I can't figure out what he meant.

Finally, if you want to change your name, you can simply do it by exercising your common law right. You need not go to court at all. (This is not true in all states, however, such as Oklahoma.) If you choose this route, the first thing to do is to start amassing identification in your new name. This is exactly what Le Elen Miller did in Idaho in the early 1970s. She was married at that time, using her husband's surname, but had decided to resume use of her birth name. She explained:

I handled the actual name change very simply. I applied for a change in my Social Security card using the regular name-change form. Then I went to the local driver's license center and asked for a form on which to report a change of name (I didn't elaborate on the purpose of the change, letting the personnel there assume I was getting married — I don't wear a wedding band). Next I went to a different bank in my city and opened a new checking account in my birth name. This sequence of events provided me with identification for check cashing locally from the beginning.

Later when I applied for credit cards, I simply left any spaces applying to marriage or spouse blank. If I felt it might be an issue, in the space for title, I would indicate (by write-in if necessary) that I prefer "Ms." to Miss. That choice probably made merchants assume I was single.

At the time that Le Elen changed her name, the Social Security office was the easiest place to get a new ID, but they now have stricter requirements. Depending on your state's regulations, the place to start may be the motor vehicle department, to get a new driver's license. Then you can use this important ID to acquire additional ones.

121

Catherine Stark Zybkun is a Wisconsin woman who recently changed her name by common law. Before she tried to get new identification, she prepared a notarized statement. (Her husband, who changed his name at the same time, also used such a statement.) Her statement read:

DECLARATION OF NAME CHANGE
I declare that I have changed my name by the common law method of consistent and non-fraudulent use. Since 24 June 1989, I have been using my new name, Catherine Stark Zybkun. I was previously known as Catherine Marie Stark.

Using the notarized statements, Catherine and her husband applied for new driver's licenses. Though the personnel at the Department of Motor Vehicles were initially a bit puzzled, they issued the new licenses with no trouble. At the Social Security office, Catherine and her husband each had to show one ID with the old name and one with the new name; this was easy, because they had the driver's licenses. They were then given new Social Security cards. At one bank where she went to change the name on her account, Catherine just had to produce an ID with her new name, and at another bank she had to show that she'd changed her Social Security records as well.

Overall, Catherine says, she was surprised at how simple it was to change her name. She recommends getting a driver's license first, because that is generally the most widely accepted form of identification. With that and her Social Security card, she expects that she will have no trouble changing other name-related materials such as credit cards.[7]

Catherine found that it is quite easy to change your name without going through the court system. To make the process run smoothly, you need to be consistent and thorough and understand that you are simply exercising a legal right.

Informing the World

Once you've chosen the name that you're going to use, how do you tell people about it? A permanent name tag ("HELLO! My name is _____") is probably not a good long-term solution! Most women just mention their names when appropriate: "Yes, I'm married now, but I kept my birth name," or "I dropped my ex-husband's name after my divorce — I'm Jane Jones again." But some feel that something a bit more formal is required. Several modern etiquette books provide suggestions.

Judith Martin, writing as "Miss Manners," suggests sending "At Home" cards with the wedding invitations. These cards state the bride's and groom's names, where they'll be "at home," and after what date.[8] (This might seem a bit quaint and old-fashioned in most circles today, but it probably would get people's attention!) Charlotte Ford says that a woman who will be using her birth name or a hyphenated name after marriage could simply enclose cards to this effect in the wedding invitations or announcements.[9]

Cathy Ann Stone Wilson, who added her husband's surname to her own, followed Ford's advice, stating in her wedding invitations that the bride had chosen to assume the name Cathy Ann Stone Wilson. "The response was very positive (even from men)," she wrote, "and it seemed to make a formal *rite du passage* for everyone. I think that helped a great deal in making the change."

If you take back your birth name or choose a new name after divorce, name-change announcements might be a good way to tell people. Charlotte Ford suggests two possible formats:

> Anne Kramer announces
> that she will be known as
> Anne Stuckey
> as of September 1, 1989

or

> Virginia Thompson
> wishes to announce
> that she will be returning to her birth given name
> Virginia Breckenridge
> for all legal and social purposes

Helen Langer, who took back her birth name sometime after being divorced, found that announcements worked well. (Her announcement was a small pink card that read: "Helen Langer Graham has resumed her own name: Helen Anne Langer.") "I sent them out with Christmas cards that year," she wrote, "and I think it was a bright idea. Everyone learned at once. I did the same to businesses, etc. as bills and notices came in."

Depending upon your inclinations and social circle, you may or may not want to send formal announcements of your name. But more important, remember that if you're changing, rather than retaining, your name, you must do the leg-, phone-, and pen-work involved in changing your name on your driver's license, voter registration, credit cards, Social Security records, health insurance, employer's records, etc. Once you've done all that, you can just sit back and enjoy using the name *you* have chosen!

13. Children's Names — The Law

Many of the women who participated in my study were concerned about naming their children. Some not only worried about what surname to give the children, but wondered what legal issues are involved. Can you give a child a name other than its father's, without having legal problems? Are there any laws that restrict parental naming rights? These questions are not simple, and the facts are often not easy to gather.

The issue of children's names is closely related to that of women's names. In fact, for some women the question "What should I name my children?" has developed out of the question "What should I name myself?" In a 1976 case involving children's names, the Washington Supreme Corut recognized this connection when it wrote, "As more women exercise their right to retain their own surname after marriage, the likelihood that children will be given a surname other than the paternal surname increases."[1]

The two issues share a basis in common law. Just as the common law acknowledges that a person may use any name he or she chooses (without intent to defraud), it acknowledges that parents may give their children any name they choose. Children born to married parents do not have to receive their father's surname, and children born to unmarried parents do not have to receive their mother's name.

During the 1970s some states passed laws to undercut parents' common law right to name their children. Hawaii, North Carolina, Florida, Louisiana, and New Hampshire required that children born to married parents receive their fathers' names. These laws have all since been repealed, replaced, or declared unconstitutional. However, some of these same states, as well as others, currently have laws that still restrict parents' rights. Some, for example, allow parents only three choices: the father's name, the mother's name, or a combination name.

Up to 15 or 20 years ago, questions of children's surnames rarely arose. Parents generally gave their children the father's surname, and

125

that was that. This situation changed in the early to mid-1970s, when women became more aware of their right to name their children. Their success in asserting this right has depended primarily upon whether the parents agree or disagree about the names to give their children.[2]

When Parents Agree

Some women, in agreement with their husbands, began giving children the mother's birth name, a hyphenated name, or even a completely new name. These parents often ran into opposition from state agencies, usually at the point when they had to register the births. Kass Sheedy and Douglas Morea, who participated in my study, gave their children a surname different from either parent: Ailanthus. They encountered problems when their children were born. Kass wrote:

> Prior to our older daughter's birth we researched the legality of the question and determined that a third surname was legal. We informed the hospital of what we were doing when I was admitted. We also informed the State Registrar (in Delaware) beforehand and met with a great deal of resistance. After numerous, very heated, phone calls the Registrar finally agreed to accept the birth certificate when the time came. We told the pediatrician and he used the proper name in his records with no problem. Despite all the preparation, when we were handed Caroline's birth certificate on the way out of the hospital it had my husband's surname. We protested (loudly) but were told that if we wanted a birth certificate, that was it. Approximately six weeks later we went to court for an official name change for her. The judge seemed rather amused and granted the change.
>
> When our second child was born (in December 1981) we again informed the hospital (same one as before) about the surname. The records people were convinced it was illegal, or at least not normal procedure. A helpful nurse gave my husband the number of an official in the state capital. He and my husband finally succeeded in convincing the hospital that we could use a third surname for the baby. Her birth certificate was issued under the name Ailanthus.

Even though they tried to be well-prepared, Kass and Douglas encountered annoying problems with state officials, particularly the state registrar. In most cases, however, registrars will record a child's name as anything the parents want, unless state law forbids it. Most couples, therefore, do not have a problem in naming their children. If they do, and take the case to court, the parents will prevail. So Kass and Douglas, though they didn't know it, could probably have fought the state of Delaware (more precisely, its state registrar) and won.

In fact, whenever parents (suing jointly) have challenged a state law or other requirement stating that a child must receive the father's name, they have won.[3] The courts feel very strongly that such laws infringe upon the rights of parents to raise their children as they wish. In an influential 1977 case, the Massachusetts Supreme Court told the city and town clerks in that state that a married couple may give their children any surname they choose.[4]

In 1979 Adolf Befurt and Alena Jech, a Hawaii couple, challenged a state law requiring that a child born of married parents be given its father's surname. Mr. Befurt and Ms. Jech wanted to give their son the surname Jebef — a combination of their surnames. When state officials would not allow this on the child's birth certificate, the parents brought suit. In its decision the federal district court specifically stated that under the United States Constitution, parents have the right to determine the names of their children.[5]

Similar decisions followed in other states. In North Carolina there was a law much like that in Hawaii, in which married parents had to give their children the father's surname. Three sets of married parents challenged it in 1981. The federal district court invalidated the law, stating that it "impinges upon decisions affecting family life, procreation, and child rearing: areas of human experience which the Supreme Court has long held must be accorded special protection."[6] In 1982, Christine Ledbetter and Dean Skylar wanted to name their son Sydney Anthony Skybetter (after Sydney Harris, Susan B. Anthony, and a fused version of the parental surnames). To do so, they challenged Florida's naming law, and were upheld by a federal court.[7]

When Parents Disagree

The situation is quite different when parents disagree on the names to give their children. This may occur if parents divorce before a child is born, or if parents divorce when the child is older and the custodial parent wants to change the child's surname. Since the mother is most often the custodial parent, it is usually she who wants to name or rename the child. Priscilla Ruth MacDougall, an expert on women's rights to name their children, has stated that if the father objects to the mother's choice of name, "a woman finds herself facing an almost insurmountable legal obstacle."[8] Until 1980, courts generally stated that the father had the right to name children (unless the parents were unmarried), if the parents could not agree. In most cases this meant that the children received or kept the father's surname.

In 1980 the California Supreme Court handed down a decision that set an important precedent. They stated in *In re Schiffman* that "the rule giving the father, as against the mother, a primary right to have his child bear his surname should be abolished."[9] Partly as a result of the *Schiffman* case, many courts have ruled favorably toward the mother in name disputes in the past several years. Others, however, have continued to uphold the fathers. Most cases where the decisions have favored the mothers involved women who had been married to the child's father, and who used their birth surnames. The children in question were all newborns or infants.

The courts have ruled differently when the children are older (over age three) and already bear their father's surnames. In these cases, the courts have almost always decided that a noncustodial father has the right to have his children bear his name, unless he has been guilty of abuse or abandonment. Many courts have also stated that keeping the father's name is in the "best interests" of the child, and that it will help to maintain the father–child bond.

It is particularly difficult for custodial mothers to change their noninfant children's surnames because the burden of proof is upon them to show definitively that it is *not* in the children's best interests to use the fathers' names. The fathers bear no such burden of proof.

Only two divorced women in my study mentioned that they gave their birth names to their children. One said that her children bore her name because she divorced when they were very young. She gave no details.

Virginia Beal took back her birth name a year or so after her divorce. (As an aside, she noted that she did not tell the court that she had a child. At that time Michigan divorce law did not permit a divorced mother to change to a name different from that of her children unless she remarried.) Sometime thereafter, she had her son's surname legally changed to hers. There's a twist to her story, too. Virginia writes, "My son had legally carried my name since age five, and unofficially since about age two, before he first knew people had more than one name.

At present, he lives with his father, who'd originally signed off and not seen him in 12 years. Father and son now have different names — talk about turnabout!"

Virginia was probably able to change her son's name without difficulty because the boy's father had denied responsibility and interest in him. Otherwise the courts would have been as reluctant to grant this type of change as they would a change to a stepfather's name.

Sharon Burcher gave a new surname to herself and her son Donald several years after her divorce. She explained that right after her divorce, she took back her birth name, O'Brien, as specified in her divorce decree. Donald continued to use his father's surname, Lane. When he started school there was a lot of confusion because mother and son had different surnames. One day Donald got sick. The school officials could not contact Sharon because of the name difference, and her parents had to drive from another city to pick up their grandson. Sharon decided this was the last straw: "That night Donald and I picked us a name out of the telephone book. We selected Burcher and I changed everything, credit cards, business cards, and even Donald's Social Security number registration."

Sharon said that when she made this change she consulted her lawyer. "He said there was nothing illegal about our changing our name — we were not hiding anything, and we were not denying that Donald is his father's son." She has not changed their name through legal proceedings because, she wrote, "I doubt that my ex-husband would consent to changing Donald's name in court. . . . Donald's father was not the least bit pleased by what I did, but there is literally nothing he can do about it, except to still call him 'Lane,' which he does." Sharon is probably fortunate that her ex-husband apparently did not feel sufficiently strongly about the matter to take her to court. Considering the judicial record in cases of this kind, he would probably have won.

Clearly, the whole subject of women's right to name their children is a tangled one. If you are a divorced mother with custody of her child, can you give the child a surname other than its father's? Your chances are fairly good if the child is a newborn, and if you want to give the child your birth surname or another suname that you did not acquire by marriage. Priscilla MacDougall believes that gradually the courts are making the presumption that the custodial parent, generally the mother, should determine a child's surname, especially when the child is a newborn or very young.

If your child is older, it's much more difficult. If your ex-husband objects to your choice of name for the child, and you take the case to court, you may well lose. In ten years or so, the situation may be different. MacDougall hopes that if enough cases of this kind are brought to court and are argued skillfully, the courts may recognize that naming of noninfant children is one of the rights of the custodial parent. "It is a fundamental women's concern," she writes, "that women who are custodial parents have the same legally recognized decision-making power respecting their children's names as they have over other aspects of their children's lives."[10]

14. Conclusion

"'*Must* a name mean something?' Alice asked doubtfully. 'Of course it must,' Humpty Dumpty said. . . . 'My name means the shape I am. . . . With a name like yours, you might be any shape, almost.'"[1]

Yes, names mean a great deal. When I first began this study, I knew they were important. I just didn't realize the depth to which they were important. Then the questionnaires started piling up in my mailbox. When I opened them, this is what women told me:

> All of my life I had been "making" me. To change my name seemed to be starting on a whole new person as well as wiping out all traces of the "me" who had accomplished, made friends, existed.

> I love my name. After 30 years of answering to other people's names, I was astonished at the deep happiness regaining my own name gives to me—simple, profound joy. I really am me again.

> I'm still glad I chose it. Psychologically it reinforces my individualism.

> It's been wonderful to finally be ME. It took over a year to find the right name and it's been nothing but UP since then.

I was startled at the intensity of their feelings. Many of the women who wrote to me felt that their names are at the core of their being. Often those who maintained their names after marriage did so with the attitude, "If I change my name, it will change who I am." And frequently a woman who adopted an entirely new name felt she had been reborn, had become a "new person." Sharon Lebell provides an explanation for this identification between name and self:

> At a preconscious level, our minds don't distinguish between the name itself and the person to whom it refers. The name and the person are one and the same. So, when we talk about changing our names, the mind

131

> hears that as changing who we are. Names are emotionally and
> spiritually powerful because we are our names and our names are us.[2]

According to this view, the relationship between name and self is initially the same for male and female children. When children grow up, men keep the same name, and therefore the same "self." Most women, however, change their surnames, and thereby undergo some change in self.

According to Lebell, because women expect to change their names, they don't have a positive association with their names and don't allow themselves to develop a fixed identity. She contends they remain too flexible, constantly altering themselves to fit circumstances. Because of this, "women lose out on the possibility of defining their personality through their actions and the public record of those actions."[3]

There is some truth to what Lebell says. When a woman changes her name, she effectively fragments her history. Assume, for example, that a woman named Jane Smith has academic degrees, publications, and professional achievements attached to her name. When she marries and becomes Jane Brown, it is more difficult for her or for others to directly retrieve her pre-marriage attributes and accomplishments. She knows or fears that this will occur, because she expects to change her name. This knowledge may deprive her of the motivation to enhance her name and reputation. Although the motivation to enhance one's name is neither sufficient or necessary for achievement, it's certainly additive.

Lebell recognizes the value of a consistent name as an incentive for achievement. However, she has probably overstated the effects of name-changing upon women. If a woman wants to, she can make impact on the world, and can be remembered for it, no matter what her name.

Names and Marriage

Nonetheless, many of the women in my study were afraid of losing themselves by changing their names. They viewed retaining their own names as indications of independence and autonomy, and they feared giving up any of this sense of being an individual. I've quoted many women, particularly in Chapters 2, 4, 6, and 7, who feel this way. Here are a few more examples:

Conclusion

> I am glad that I maintained my birth name — the idea of being married was threatening to me and using my husband's name would have made me feel as if I had lost my identity as an individual.

> It's the only name with which I could be comfortable. I would feel degraded if I had to play second class citizen to a man and treat his name as if it were better than mine and thus the one to use upon marriage.

> In an intangible, personal sense, the different surname helps me to maintain a sense of separateness, financially and emotionally. I loathe any implication of dependence or subordinate/superior relationships between husband and wife. Such does not exist in our marriage; however, the different surnames seem to confirm (rather than aid in establishing) this characteristic in our marriage.

> My husband and I see me as an individual, not as his appendage. I do not want what he does to reflect on me and vice versa. We are separate individuals. I do not want him to feel obligated to be responsible for my life.

I think that to a large extent these feelings have grown out of the ideas of the women's movement of the past 20 years. These ideas, sometimes justifiably, emphasized men as oppressors of women, and marriage as a "prison" for women. They told women that they can best fulfill themselves and "be all they can be" by maintaining as much independence as possible from men. Attitudes like these still appear in some feminist writing today. For example, in discussing marriage as a cornerstone of patronymic, Lebell writes:

> Marriage is not union, and two do not become one flesh. It is two discrete individuals going together on a mutual life journey.... Since in reality two can't really become one, something has to give, *someone* has to give, and that someone is the woman. Males can wax rhapsodic about this union business because they don't give anything up. When women marry, they give up an elemental part of their identity in service of building up their husband's.[4]

The questionnaire responses that I received indicate that many well-educated women who grew up in the late 1960s and the 1970s have carried the ideas from the women's movement into their own relationships. They felt they had to assert their autonomy *vis-à-vis* men and not become subjugated. Yet they did not abandon marriage. All of the

133

women in the study have been married, and most were married at the time of the study. However, many seemed to be hesitant to make certain commitments to their marriages. For many, the "name issue" was simply a window through which they revealed their conflict between autonomy and commitment.

It's Your Choice

I titled this book *Surnames for Women* because choice is what it's all about. A woman doesn't have to take the traditional route of adopting her husband's name upon marriage. She has a whole range of options — keeping her birth name, hyphenating her surname with her husband's, taking an old family name, creating a new name, and so on. The women in this book have all made one of these choices, and in general they've been very pleased with what they've done. Most of them, though not all, have been able to find the name that is right for them.

For some women, the right decision is to take their husbands' surnames. This is the choice with which they're most comfortable. I questioned a few women (comparable in age and education to the participants in my study) who had taken their husbands' names. A 27-year-old homemaker with one child told me, "I'm proud of it [my husband's name]. I wouldn't have it any other way. I guess I might be old-fashioned in that sense. He is my husband and I'm proud to bear his name." Another explained, "It would be too inconvenient and confusing to have a different name from my husband. Also, I like to do things in a conventional way." This attitude was not unanimous, however. One woman said, "I felt I lost my identity as an individual when I took my husband's name," and another said, "I wish I had kept my maiden name. I would change back except for the professional and legal complications and hassle." On the whole, though, the women who used their husbands' surnames were happy with their decisions. Like their husbands (quoted in Chapter 7), and in fact like most of the people in this study, they tended to support and justify the decisions they had made.

I feel strongly that one's name should be a personal choice. Just as a woman shouldn't feel guilty if she chooses to be a homemaker with children instead of a nuclear physicist, she shouldn't feel guilty or feel like a "traitor to the feminist cause" if she chooses to take her husband's surname. The women's movement, after all, should be concerned with choices, not ultimatums. Hanna Holborn Gray, president of the University of Chicago, discussed the women's movement and its influence on young women in an interview in mid-1988. What she said can be applied to names as well as to many other issues facing women: "I would say to young women on campuses today, 'Remember that what the women's liberation movement ought to be about is liberating you, giving you choices to make, and don't let people seduce you into thinking that there's only one choice you can make.'"[5]

As a woman in my study wrote, "I think women should be encouraged to do with their name whatever they feel is appropriate in their situation. This isn't a crusade for me. It's like the choice to be married or single. There's no one correct answer." Most important, women should know that they *have* choices in the names they use.

Notes

Introduction

1. Mary Lassiter, *Our Names, Our Selves: The Meaning of Names in Everyday Life* (London: Heinemann, 1983), p. 81.
2. Susan Deller Ross, *The Rights of Women: The Basic ACLU Guide to a Woman's Rights* (New York: Avon, 1973), p. 254.
3. Ruth Hale, *The First Five Years of the Lucy Stone League* (New York: Lucy Stone League, [1926]), pp. 9–10.
4. Priscilla Ruth MacDougall, "The Right of Women to Name Their Children," *Law and Inequality: A Journal of Theory and Practice* 3, p. 95.

Chapter 1. A Short History of Women's Names in America

1. Elizabeth L. Post, *Emily Post's Etiquette* (New York: Harper & Row, 1984).
2. Editors of *Bride's* Magazine with Susan D. Hackman, *The New Bride's Book of Etiquette* (New York: Grosset & Dunlap, 1981), p. 49.
3. Una Stannard, *Mrs. Man* (San Francisco: Germainbooks, 1977), p. 35. In this chapter I have also used some other examples of well-known and lesser-known American women from Stannard's book.
4. Elisabeth Griffith, *In Her Own Right: The Life of Elizabeth Cady Stanton* (New York: Oxford University Press, 1984), p. xx.
5. Leslie Wheeler, ed., *Loving Warriors: Selected Letters of Lucy Stone and Henry B. Blackwell, 1853 to 1893* (New York: Dial, 1981), p. 3.
6. *Ibid.*, p. 163.
7. *Ibid.*, p. 259.
8. June Sochen, *Movers and Shakers: American Women Thinkers and Activists, 1900–1970* (New York: Quadrangle, 1973), p. 4.
9. *Ibid.*, p. 91.
10. Hale, *The First Five Years of the Lucy Stone League*, pp. 14–17.
11. *People ex rel Rago v. Lipsky*, 327 Ill. App. 63, 63 N.E.2d 642 (1945).
12. *Bucher v. Brower*, 21 Ohio Op. 208, 7 Ohio Supp. 51 (1941).
13. *Krupa v. Green*, 114 Ohio App. 497, 177 N.E.2d 616 (1961).
14. *Forbush v. Wallace*, 341 F. Supp. 217 (M.D. Ala. 1971); affirmed *per curiam* by the U.S. Supreme Court, 415 U.S. 970 (1972).

15. *Stuart v. Board of Supervisors of Elections for Howard County*, 266 Md. 440, 295 A.2d 223 (1972).

Chapter 2. Identity

1. Lassiter, *Our Names, Our Selves*, preface.
2. Erik Erikson, *Identity: Youth and Crisis* (New York: Norton, 1968), pp. 22–23.
3. *Detroit News*, 28 July 1982.
4. Harvey Stein, *Artists Observed* (New York: Abrams, 1986). Lee Krasner did not participate in my study.

Chapter 3. Family Ties

1. Jane Howard, *Families* (New York: Simon & Schuster, 1978), pp. 29–30.

Chapter 4. Feminism and Politics

1. This is an excerpt from NOW's Statement of Purpose, adopted at the Organizational Conference on October 29, 1966. Quoted in Carol Hymowitz and Michaele Weissman, *A History of Women in America* (New York: Bantam, 1978), p. 344.
2. David Bouchier, *The Feminist Challenge: The Movement for Women's Liberation in Britain and the U.S.A.* (New York: Schocken, 1983), p. 219.
3. Karen DeCrow, *Sexist Justice* (New York: Random House, 1974), p. 250.
4. Gene Marine, *A Male Guide to Women's Liberation* (New York: Holt, Rinehart & Winston, 1972), p. 232.
5. Erica Jong, "The Artist as Housewife," in *The First Ms. Reader*, ed. Francine Klagsbrun (New York: Warner, 1972), pp. 113–114.
6. Sharon Lebell, *Naming Ourselves, Naming Our Children: Resolving the Last Name Dilemma* (Freedom, Calif.: Crossing, 1988), p. 28.
7. Bouchier, *The Feminist Challenge*, p. 197.
8. Betty Friedan, *The Second Stage* (New York: Summit, 1981), p. 31.
9. *Ibid.*, p. 36.

Chapter 5. Pragmatism

1. *Chicago Tribune*, 22 November 1981.
2. *Washington Post*, 24 February 1983.

Notes

Chapter 9. Naming the Children

1. Lebell, *Naming Ourselves, Naming Our Children*, p. 27.
2. *Ibid.*, pp. 63–66.

Chapter 10. Problems in Business and Government

1. Glen Walker, *Credit Where Credit Is Due: A Legal Guide to Your Credit Rights and How to Assert Them* (New York: Holt, Rinehart & Winston, 1979), pp. 44–46.
2. *Ibid.*, p. 46.
3. *Ibid.*, p. 54.

Chapter 11. Other Problems

1. *Washington Post*, 15 July 1988.

Chapter 12. Women's Names — The Law

1. MacDougall, "The Right of Women to Name Their Children," p. 105.
2. *The Capital Times* (Madison, Wisconsin), 31 July 1973.
3. *Kruzel v. Podell,* 67 Wis. 2d 138, 226 N.W. 2d 458 (1975).
4. MacDougall, "The Right of Women to Name Their Children," p. 96. In a footnote on pp. 96–98 MacDougall lists the relevant legislation, court decisions, etc., in each state.
5. *North Carolina General Statutes*, Sections 50–12 and 101–1 through 101–8.
6. *In re Mohlman*, 26 N.C. App. 220, 216 S.E. 2d 147 (1975).
7. This information is from a letter from Catherine Stark Zybkun to Priscilla Ruth MacDougall, July 1989. I thank MacDougall for sharing this document with me. (Catherine Stark Zybkun is not her real name.)
8. Judith Martin, *Miss Manners' Guide to Excruciatingly Correct Behavior* (New York: Atheneum, 1982), p. 333.
9. Charlotte Ford, *Etiquette — Charlotte Ford's Guide to Modern Manners* (New York: Potter, 1988), p. 267.

Chapter 13. Children's Names — The Law

1. *Doe v. Dunning*, 87 Wash. 2d 50, 53, 549, P.2d 1, 3 (1976).
2. The major legal work on children's names is Priscilla Ruth MacDougall's article, "The Right of Women to Name Their Children." Much of the information in this chapter is based upon her detailed and exhaustive article.

3. MacDougall, "The Right of Women to Name Their Children," p. 117.

4. *Secretary of the Commonwealth v. City Clerk of Lowell*, 373 Mass. 178, 366 N.E. 2d 717 (1977).

5. *Jech v. Burch*, 466 F. Supp. 714 (D. Hawaii 1979).

6. *O'Brien v. Tilson*, 523 F. Supp. 494 (E.D.N.C. 1981).

7. *Sydney v. Pingree* 564 F. Supp. 412 (S.D. Fla. 1982).

8. MacDougall, "The Right of Women to Name Their Children," p. 99.

9. *In re Schiffman*, 28 Cal. 3d 640, 620 P.2d 579, 169 Cal Rptr. 918 (1980).

10. MacDougall, "The Right of Women to Name Their Children," p. 100.

Chapter 14. Conclusion

1. Lewis Carroll, *Through the Looking Glass*, in *Complete Works of Lewis Carroll* (New York: Random House, 1936), p. 209.

2. Lebell, *Naming Ourselves, Naming Our Children*, p. 7.

3. *Ibid.*, p. 25.

4. *Ibid.*, pp. 37–38.

5. Leslie Maitland Werner, "The Gray Presidency – The First Ten Years," *The University of Chicago Magazine* 81:10.

Bibliography

Ashley, Leonard R.N. "Changing Times and Changing Names: Reasons, Regulations and Rights." *Names* **19**:167–187.

Baldrige, Letitia. *Amy Vanderbilt's Everyday Etiquette.* New York: Bantam, 1981.

Bouchier, David. *The Feminist Challenge: The Movement for Women's Liberation in Britain and the U.S.A.* New York: Schocken, 1983.

Cameron, Catherine. *The Name Givers—How They Influence Your Life.* Englewood Cliffs, N.J.: Prentice Hall, 1983.

Carroll, Lewis. *Through the Looking Glass.* In *Complete Works of Lewis Carroll* (New York: Random House, 1936).

DeCrow, Karen. *Sexist Justice.* New York: Random House, 1974.

Dion, Kenneth L. "Names, Identity and Self." *Names* **31**: 245–257.

Editors of *Bride's* Magazine with Hackman, Susan D. *The New Bride's Book of Etiquette.* New York: Grosset and Dunlap, 1981.

Erikson, Erik. *Identity: Youth and Crisis.* New York: Norton, 1968.

————. *Identity and the Life Cycle.* New York: Norton, 1959.

Ford, Charlotte. *Etiquette—Charlotte Ford's Guide to Modern Manners.* New York: Potter, 1988.

Friedan, Betty. *The Second Stage.* New York: Summit, 1981.

Griffith, Elisabeth. *In Her Own Right: The Life of Elizabeth Cady Stanton.* New York: Oxford University Press, 1984.

Hale, Ruth. *The First Five Years of the Lucy Stone League.* New York: The Lucy Stone League, [1926].

Hays, Elinor Rice. *Morning Star: A Biography of Lucy Stone 1818–1893.* New York: Harcourt, Brace and World, 1961.

Hirsch, Barbara B. *Living Together: A Guide to the Law for Unmarried Couples.* Boston: Houghton Mifflin, 1976.

Howard, Jane. *Families.* New York: Simon & Schuster, 1978.

Hymowitz, Carol, and Weissman, Michaele. *A History of Women in America.* New York: Bantam, 1978.

Jong, Erica. "The Artist as Housewife." In *The First Ms. Reader,* edited by Francine Klagsbrun. New York: Warner, 1972.

Kanowitz, Leo. *Sex Roles in Law and Society: Cases and Materials.* Albuquerque: University of New Mexico Press, 1973.

————. *Women and the Law: The Unfinished Revolution.* Albuquerque: University of New Mexico Press, 1969.

141

Lakoff, Robin. *Language and Woman's Place*. New York: Harper and Row, 1975.

Lassiter, Mary. *Our Names, Our Selves: The Meaning of Names in Everyday Life*. London: Heinemann, 1983.

Lebell, Sharon. *Naming Ourselves, Naming Our Children: Resolving the Last Name Dilemma*. Freedom, Calif.: Crossing, 1988.

Lerner, Gerda. "Placing Women in History: Definitions and Challenges." In *The Majority Finds Its Past: Placing Women in History*. New York: Oxford University Press, 1979.

_____. "Women's Rights and American Feminism." In *The Majority Finds Its Past: Placing Women in History*. New York: Oxford University Press, 1979.

MacDougall, Priscilla Ruth. "Married Women's Common Law Right to Their Own Surnames." *Women's Rights Law Reporter* 1:2–14.

_____. "The Right of Women to Name Their Children." *Law and Inequality: A Journal of Theory and Practice* 3: 91–159.

Marine, Gene. *A Male Guide to Women's Liberation*. New York: Holt, Rinehart and Winston, 1972.

Martin, Judith. *Miss Manners' Guide to Excruciatingly Correct Behavior*. New York: Atheneum, 1982.

Miller, Casey, and Swift, Kate. *Words and Women*. Garden City, N.Y.: Anchor, 1976.

Plicque, Anne M.M. "Keeping My Own Name." *Essence* 16: 151.

Post, Elizabeth L. *Emily Post's Etiquette*. New York: Harper & Row, 1984.

Rennick, Robert M. "Judicial Procedures for a Change-of-Name in the U.S." *Names* 13:145–168.

_____. "On the Right of Exclusive Possession of a Family Name." *Names* 32:138–155.

Rosenwein, Rivka. "What's in a Surname? Genealogists Fear Family-Tree Trouble." *Wall Street Journal*, 11 February 1987.

Ross, Susan Deller. *The Rights of Women: The Basic ACLU Guide to a Woman's Rights*. New York: Avon, 1973.

Rossi, Alice S. *The Feminist Papers: From Adams to de Beauvoir*. New York: Columbia University Press, 1973.

Slovenko, Ralph. "Overview: Names and the Law." *Names* 32:107–113.

Sochen, June. *Herstory: A Record of the American Woman's Past*. Sherman Oaks, Calif.: Alfred, 1981.

_____. *Movers and Shakers: American Women Thinkers and Activists, 1900–1970*. New York: Quadrangle, 1973.

Stannard, Una. *Married Women v. Husbands' Names: The Case for Wives Who Keep Their Own Name*. San Francisco: Germainbooks, 1973.

_____. *Mrs. Man*. San Francisco: Germainbooks, 1977.

Stein, Harvey. *Artists Observed*. New York: Abrams, 1986.

Switzer, Ellen, *The Law for a Woman: Real Cases and What Happened*. New York: Scribner's, 1971.

Walker, Glen. *Credit Where Credit Is Due: A Legal Guide to Your Credit*

Bibliography

Rights and How to Assert Them. New York: Holt, Rinehart and Winston, 1979.

Warwick, Donald P., and Lininger, Charles A. *The Sample Survey: Theory and Practice.* New York: McGraw-Hill, 1975.

Werner, Leslie Maitland. "The Gray Presidency — The First Ten Years." *The University of Chicago Magazine* 81.

Wheeler, Leslie, ed. *Loving Warriors: Selected Letters of Lucy Stone and Henry B. Blackwell, 1853 to 1893.* New York: Dial, 1981.

Index

Index